SOS YOUR LIFE

The RoadMap for
Purpose-Driven Individuals to
Navigate Their Way Back to
Their Own Best Life

Sara Southey

SOS YOUR LIFE

The RoadMap for Purpose-Driven Individuals to Navigate Their Way Back to Their Own Best Life

© 2025 Sara Southey, Director The Southey Way Ltd.

All rights reserved. No part of this book may be reproduced, stored in a retrieval system or transmitted in any form or by any means (electronic, mechanical, photocopy, recording, scanning or other) except for brief quotations in critical reviews or articles, without the prior written permission of the publisher.

ISBN: 9781068277009 Paperback

Published by: Inspired By Publishing

The strategies in this book are presented primarily for enjoyment and educational purposes. Every effort has been made to trace copyright holders and obtain their permission for the use of copyright material.

The information and resources provided in this book are based upon the authors' personal experiences. Any outcome, income statements or other results, are based on the authors' experiences and there is no guarantee that your experience will be the same. There is an inherent risk in any business enterprise or activity and there is no guarantee that you will have similar results as the author as a result of reading this book.

The author reserves the right to make changes and assumes no responsibility or liability whatsoever on behalf of any purchaser or reader of these materials.

Dedication

For my mother–

Literally and literarily,
the greatest influence on and in my life.

Never not with me.

Foreword

Sara used to introduce herself in business settings as "not just a personal trainer." Under normal circumstances, I am not a huge fan of the word "just" as it is usually associated with a huge dollop of self-deprecation and a misunderstanding of personal and professional brilliance. However, in Sara's case, the "just" is to help others who may have made some assumptions about her understand that these assumptions may have been misplaced.

Sara is a magnificent personal trainer, but that is only one facet of her expertise. I have had the honour and pleasure of working with Sara and consider her a deeply intelligent, highly skilled, empathic human being, and a dear and precious friend.

I can't tell you how pleased I am that she has finally put pen to paper; it's been in the pipeline for a long time! This is a book I am confident will have something of value to offer everyone, so buy some copies for your friends and colleagues. They will be forever grateful. Why? Because, however well developed we consider ourselves to be, there are times when life throws us a googly. For those unfamiliar with this cricketing term: a googly is a type of bowling delivery – also known as a wrong'un" – that takes an unexpected direction and often catches the batter off guard!

There is nobody I would rather have in my corner than Sara when I need help sorting out my sh*t, having been on the receiving end of many of life's googlies! Her practical, compassionate, individualised approach, together with her deep knowledge and vast experience, means that she tailors her support so that it fits like a glove.

Changing habits that no longer serve us means that we also have to alter the way we think and behave to get the best outcomes. Sara shares her story as a way of lighting our path. We can take what is useful to each of us and leave what isn't! What is fascinating to me is that what readers need and take from this book may be different for each. I know it will be a book that I return to often, as I suspect those googlies will revisit in many forms over time. I know that I can dip back into the relevant chapters as needed. That is a testament to great writing.

Thank you, Sara, for asking me to write this foreword. All that remains is to encourage you to prepare to write your next one!

Dr. Jenny Gordon
PhD, BSc, RGN, RSCN
Founder & Director of Jenuine Consulting Ltd.

Jenny is based in Oxfordshire, serving the world.

She is a doyenne of misunderstood brilliance, powered by JENERGY, the essence of her own unique brilliance, reclaimed over many decades; she uses hers to activate yours.

A proud mum, nanny, aunt, cousin, friend, confidante; embracing the powerful platinum phase of her life with joy, passion and purposeful presence. So much still to become and do.

She is a personality-powered leadership coach with a background in healthcare. Drawing on her extensive life experience and scientific training, combined with her doctoral expertise, she brings a wealth of insight that she has applied in various sectors, including engineering, finance, healthcare, retail and education.

She helps entrepreneurs be bolder, braver and brighter by creating clarity and confidence from deep self-awareness. She brings passionate disruption to the status quo and provokes new perspectives, encouraging people to rediscover and reconnect with their potential and increase their influence by understanding themselves, so they can share their unique brilliance in all spheres of their lives.

"You can't go back and change the beginning, but you can start where you are and change the ending."

– C.S. Lewis

Contents

Introduction	1
Part 1: GroundWork A to Now	25
GroundWork: The A to Z Map of Your World	27
A to Now: Are You Currently Thriving?	45
Who Are You?	59
How Are You?	77
Part 1: A to Now Wrap Up	101
Part 2: Where Could You Go? Now to Z	109
Where Are You on the RoadMap of Life?	113
What is Your Agenda?	125
Look to the Future	139

How Do You See Yourself?	151
Your BestLife: Past, Present and Future	161
Your BestLife: What Does It Look Like?	187
Part 2: Now to Z Wrap-Up	201
Part 3: Your BestLife RoadMap	207
RoadMap: Route Planning	209
RoadMap: Choosing Your Route	219
RoadMap: Navigating your Route	229
Part 4: Your BestLife Journey	259
Just Breathe	261
Your Plan, Your Action, Your Way	265
BestLife RoadMap Wrap-Up	269
What Happens Next?	275
Acknowledgements	281

Introduction

What is your BestLife?

When was the last time you took the time to decide what your "best life" looks like?

Hand on heart, can you honestly say you have looked at all aspects of your life and chosen your actions consciously?

Most people can't.

Most people live their lives according to what is expected of them, living by their cultural norms.

Most people live in the Comfort Zone Box, and it's not one of their choosing.

When you run your own business or have a driving purpose, life can become super challenging.

You are driven to succeed in your business or purpose, *and* you have all the boxes of normality to tick.

Best-case scenario: You keep driving forward and juggling all the things, without ever feeling like you are doing any of them as well as you could. Or any of the things you actually want!

Worst-case scenario: You break down, crash and burn, and all the things you've been juggling come crashing to the floor.

Doesn't sound like much of a life, does it?

I created this BestLife RoadMap to help you sort out the shit that isn't working for you. With this road map, you can choose to start living your best life now and for the rest of your life.

The BestLife RoadMap will enable you to:

- Take responsibility for your life choices
- Take charge of what you actually want

- Choose your focus and your actions
- Use your valuable time and energy on only the things that matter.

This way, you and the important people around you get to enjoy your journey through life. The BestLife RoadMap provides you with the skills and framework needed to let go of elements in your life that are not serving. Those elements prevent you from living your best life and serving others with your purpose and business.

Sounds much better than making do or crashing and burning out, right?

Every person is different; each life is different. You and everyone you know has shit going on in life, throughout life. Only you know the combination of all those things and the importance of all those things. The choices you make will be different from the choices made by those around you. The key to living your Best Life is having your own plan, a RoadMap, that is personal and individual to you, that works for you, that flexes and adjusts as you continue living the best way you can.

This BestLife RoadMap helps you create Your Plan, Your Action, Your Way for Your Life.

I know it is a cliché, but life *is* a journey. And you get to choose and navigate your own way through it. Imagine your life as the alphabet. It is a journey from A to Z, with "A" being the day you were born and "Z" being the day you die. All the other letters in between are your journey. You have no control over when A happens, and chances are, you have no control over when Z will happen either! Here's the good news: You have control over all the other letters.

So let's make sure you are living all those in-between letters as well as you can right now – and having fun whilst you live them!

This book will help you SOS your life and provide you with your own A to Z RoadMap to live your best life, *for* life. Just like those old A to Z RoadMaps that used to hang out in the back of the car, the BestLife RoadMap is designed to travel with you through life. You can check in on your life regularly and choose which destinations you want to visit and which roads you will travel to get there.

We are humans of our own making. Yes, things happen to us that we can't control. That's just part of the journey. But the beauty of this life is you are in the driver's seat, and you get to choose *all* your actions, even the ones where you choose to do nothing! Once you realise and own this,

Introduction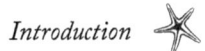

anything is possible. No matter where in your life you are, you are in control.

Now I do know that sometimes it doesn't feel like that. I mean, you wouldn't be here reading this if your life were the greatest it could be! And unfortunately, that is life; sometimes the unforeseen happens. But once you have your BestLife RoadMap in place, all the curve balls and any shit hitting the fan will be a lot easier to cope with. The solutions that work for you will be easier to find and implement.

If you have decided that your life needs to change – in whatever way you need for you to thrive – then all the work you do, including the work you'll do in this book, will ultimately be the best thing you ever choose to do for yourself!

This book will give you the RoadMap to create, plan and live your best life. It will also help you become continuously aware of *how* you are thriving on a short, medium and long-term basis.

It's important to give yourself the time and space to explore what your BestLife looks like. If you don't know what it looks like, you will never be able to live it. You will continue to live according to the expectations and influences of other people. Doesn't sound like much fun, does it? And what a waste of the opportunity to live your life to the full and enjoy as many moments as you can.

Most people don't have the time in their lives to explore what their best life looks like.

Most people carry on doing the same thing they have always done.

Most people don't consciously choose what they're doing.

Most people fall into a rut and stay there, often because it's not dreadful enough to change!

Don't be most people.

Be unapologetically you and live your life the same way!

Imagine the difference in your happiness and levels of fulfilment if you choose, right now, to live according to your own beliefs, dreams, aspirations, purpose, values.

Just by picking one of those right now and changing it, your life would be better.

So what are you waiting for?

Introduction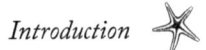

Now is *your* time.

This book is your space to think, dream, plan and change.

This is your white space in your diary, your chance to pause and breathe, your opportunity to spend time on you, your life and what you want it to look like.

We will go through the tools I personally use, as well as those I use with all my clients, for checking in with yourself. When the curveballs happen, you can check in and figure out exactly what you can do next.

I have two core values that are really, really close to my heart. It is so important that I share these with you, as they are the reason for what I do and why I'm writing this book.

The first core value: I like to leave everybody a little bit better off than I found them.

When something in this book helps make your life a little better, that fills my soul and helps me fulfil my personal purpose: to help the world thrive one person at a time. This purpose drives every action I take with my family and friends, my communities, my business, The Southey Way, with my SOS Life, Health and PT Academies – with the whole of my being.

My second core value, which I feel is just as important, is that I truly believe adulting is overrated. We need to be adults only when necessary.

The rest of our lives should be about having fun and enjoying every moment.

When you take life too seriously all the time, it tends not to have many laughs and joyous moments. I choose to "adult" only when I have to, and not the rest of the time, to ensure plenty of joy and laughter in my life!

For most of our lives, we are encouraged to grow up, take responsibility and do what is expected. How much of your time is spent doing serious, dull or mundane things? And how much is spent doing fun, silly things? My mission is to help change that percentage so that most of your life is fun and you cull out any unnecessary dullness or obligations.

Living a more vibrant life and having more fun is the ultimate goal.

You only have one life, and it should be a fun one!

(A little note about the word "should": I am going to use it in this particular case, even though normally, I'm very anti "should" because it is a word that controls our behaviour.

Introduction

It normally comes from an external source, like someone telling us what we "should" do. But this little word controls us even when we say it to ourselves! It's one of my red-flag words because when I hear it said, from an external or internal voice, it means I need to check in on myself and ask, "Why should I?" I highly recommend you practise listening for where this word is used and asking yourself the same question. Do not "should" all over yourself or your life!)

The whole SOS Your Life – BestLife RoadMap is designed with those two core values of mine in mind.

It is interactive. It is *not* going to be me telling you how you should live your life.

I will offer guiding principles and tools, some of which you may think are a little outside of the normal way of thinking. I like to twist things and make them work for me. I have written this in a way that allows you to do the same. It's more fun and your choices are more effective when you make it your own and do it your way.

This is why my company is called The Southey Way. I like to do things my way, and I help you do it your way. I do believe in thinking outside of the box, because life is really dull in the box. If you constantly live inside your box, it's predictable, safe and in your comfort zone – but nothing new or different happens. When you lift up that lid on your box, even by the littlest bit, you can discover marvellous new things and your true opportunities. That's a win for you and your best life.

Nothing may pop up as instantly relevant to you while reading this book. I understand that. If and when that happens, ask yourself, "What can I take from this? How can I twist this and reshape it into something that *is* relevant for me and my life?"

There will always be something that you can take and put into your BestLife RoadMap, if you are open to thinking differently.

Please read with an open mind. When you hear yourself think, "Yeah, but…" use it as a little warning flag in your head. Stop and pause. Ask yourself, "Is there something within myself that I'm holding on to?"

Be honest with yourself and open to new ideas and ways of thinking. That's where an opportunity for choice and change can happen, moving you closer towards your fun and thriving best life.

So, who the hell am I to help you?

Introduction

Well, I'm a person who has experienced quite a lot in life, both professionally and personally. I've had more jobs than most people have had hot dinners. I will share more of my personal story as we go through the book together. To start, let's look at the diverse jobs and careers I had from 1986 to 2016, when I started The Southey Way. It is important you know my background and how it has influenced my work, my purpose and my life.

Here's a brief snapshot:

I left school at 16 with 11 GCSEs/O Levels, as they were then, an A/O Level, and 3 shoddy A Levels in English, Maths and Russian. If you are wondering how I completed my A levels at 16, it is because I attended secondary school a year and a half earlier than most, having taken my 11+ exam at the age of 9. My grades reflect how much I disliked organised study and education. My ability to learn by doing and my common sense were always higher than showing off my intelligence and ability!

I had six months at Bristol Polytechnic, now the University of West of England, studying Systems Design (designing the machines that go "ping"). Again, not a logical choice for a non-academic. But my career teacher had told me not to bother going to University, as I would never make anything of myself, so I stuck two fingers up at her by signing up for the first course that would have me. Then I lasted six months before recognising I was not in the right place for me and my talents.

What next? I turned down a trainee accounting role I was offered because I felt it was too dull. I've never been money-motivated. Even at 16 years old, I already knew this fact about myself. In hindsight, knowing the whys and wherefores around accounting may have helped me in the three companies I've run!

In 1986, I got my first proper job at 16 years old as a typist and *then* taught myself how to type. This, after refusing a secretarial course my mother told me to do "as a backup." Sometimes, mothers do know best and 16-year-olds do not!

At 17, I set up a recruitment company without knowing how because my boss asked me to and I love a challenge. I then ran the two jobs side by side until 1991. Nobody told me I couldn't, and there was nobody else to do it. So why not?

Between the ages of 20 and 24, I was a secretary in PR, a temp in various companies and industries and an office equipment lease coordinator. Clearly, I didn't have much of a clue what I wanted to do!

Introduction

At 25, I trained and qualified as an HR professional. In those days, it was called personnel! I quickly discovered the HR profession wasn't for me, but I loved the people aspects of training and coaching. I then spent two years moving quickly through the ranks, from admin, project manager to trainer and coach for an outplacement company, which I absolutely loved. Finally, I thought, something that floated my boat.

The years 1997 to 1998 were spent as a trainer in an IT company, which involved, among other responsibilities, visiting corporates throughout the UK to learn their bespoke IT systems, writing their courses and training their teams on their software. I delivered key learning and development skills alongside training.

From 1999 to 2004, I was in the USA with my husband. As I was not allowed to work much within companies due to my visa, I did unpaid work delivering and raising my two kids!

I stayed home to raise our two beautiful, demanding and time-consuming children until 2016. While raising our kids the best way I knew how, from 2006 onwards, I also ran three consecutive businesses in gardening and garden design and build!

In 2016, I retrained and set up The Southey Way, helping purpose-driven individuals and business owners live their best lives.

My favourite role in the world (before The Southey Way) was my outplacement role. It was at a time when the Ministry of Defence was making people redundant. Thousands of people were losing what they thought was their job for life, and they were devastated. They might not have been truly happy in their job, but they were even more unhappy about losing it.

The company I worked for set targets to secure another job for these individuals within three months. Our team set our own target of getting them their *best* job within the same timeframe. Seeing these people go from utterly devastated to feeling that this was the best thing that ever happened to them, and then watching them get to do all the things they loved was incredible. It cemented my purpose and desire to help people. This purpose has stayed with me throughout the years!

When we moved to America in 1999, and I wasn't allowed to work, I had two tiny children and no separate identity from them. I even lost my name. I was just called "Mom" by everybody! On our return to the UK, the lack of identity continued; I was still "Mum." I didn't realise I was

Introduction

hugely depressed at that point. I just felt like I was failing at everything. I call this time in my life my "black years." I could barely find my way through the darkness. I had to pull myself out of that particular road and find another path.

It was bloody hard because I couldn't find anybody to support me as I went through that journey. There were a lot of people who wanted to tell me what I should and shouldn't do. But I'm not someone who responds well to this. Often, it results in me making the opposite decisions, which are not where I want to be going either!

By recognising this part of me, I knew I had to find my own way. I couldn't find the right person to help me find my way. So instead, I used all the skills I had developed and learned throughout my eclectic career and navigated my own way. It took a lot of trial and error. It took time, patience and resilience. But I knew it was as possible for me as it had been for all those we helped through their job redundancy. From 2006 to 2016, I worked on redirecting my life from merely existing to *truly* living.

After I made it through my black years, I realised I was now in the position to become the person I had been looking for back in 2006. My life experiences have pretty much given me the foundations, the knowledge and qualifications to deliver the services I now offer through my SOS Life Health and PT Academies. I can now help business owners and purpose-driven individuals live their best lives.

I set up The Southey Way and wrote this book because you don't have to face challenging times alone. I haven't found another RoadMap for life that offers the same flexibility for anyone to apply it in their own unique way.. And I absolutely refuse to put my name on anything cookie-cutter, one-size-fits-all. We are not all one size, and no one thing can fit us all. However, since 2016, I have been helping individuals navigate their way physically, mentally and emotionally and have found a way to enable them and you to discover and live the best life.

The Southey Way was created in 2016. Now, this book marks the third evolution since its founding of how we help driven business owners and purpose-led individuals sort out their shit and live their best lives, body mind and soul! Evolving, growing and thriving along this joyous road called life is one of the greatest joys and privileges you can give yourself. Having fun whilst you live is the glorious sunshine on the road!

Introduction

Why do you want to SOS your life?

This is a super important question to ask yourself.

You have picked up this book because something inside you pulled you to it.

Now is your chance to look at that something and see if we can get some clarity around *why* you want to SOS your life.

By now, you are probably realising this book isn't going to give you all the answers!

It is not a cheat sheet to life. That would be doing you a disservice.

Only you know you. Only you know your life and the dynamics that are involved in it. If there were a magic wand to make it all better, it would probably just force us into someone else's version of what a thriving life looks like.

So buckle up, open your mind and get ready to do the work you deserve to do to get your best life! It is worth every painful, uncomfortable moment. I know this because I have been through it myself. I'm still going through it and will be going through it for the rest of my life! I needed to SOS my life because something had to change. And I continue to

SOS my life because I am worth checking in on. I deserve to choose my own direction at every step of the road.

In 2006, I was at a crossroads in my life. The box I was living in had its lid well and truly welded on. I was stuck inside. The road I was on was a trudge-driven road with dark edges. To everyone around me, friends and family, I looked happy. Internally, I felt I was failing at life and was thoroughly miserable, overwhelmed and severely depressed. But I was still functioning according to the "normal" measures of living. Nobody else was neglected whilst I was going through this. Everyone was looked after except me.

I remember once thinking whilst driving on the dual carriageway to the food shop, "If you just drove off the road into the ditch, nobody would notice." I didn't want to act on the thought, but the fact that it had even entered my mind terrified me and led to me staying in more and more. On a visit to the GP about something completely separate, I struggled to hold back the tears and keep a brave face. My GP diagnosed me with depression and gave me antidepressants. This, for me, took the rollercoaster of emotions away. I remember not feeling very much at all. On the one hand, this was good because the extreme lows weren't registering. But neither did any of the highs! I felt like all the joy had been sucked out of my life.

Introduction

Even with medication, my anxiety and depression caused me to hit rock bottom. I had a moment of clarity: I was at a fork in the road and had to make a choice. One path was looking even darker and bleaker. I had no idea where the other went, but I felt it led to the light. I had to make a decision. I chose the light path. Even though I didn't know where it would take me, it was definitely a better option than the dark path!

At this point, I started to look for someone or something to help me find my way. I remember Googling all sorts of things. But at no point did I find what I was looking for. What I wanted was for someone to help me to refind *my* path and guide me back to living *my* life in a way that worked for *me*. I couldn't find the right person.

So I started by myself. Step by step, I worked it out on my own. What did and didn't work for me. It was hard and lonely work.

What didn't work for me: antidepressants, meditation, gratitude journaling, therapy, life coaching, goal-setting and planning the next five years.

What did work for me: physical movement, in tiny steps.

For someone who wasn't leaving the house unless I had to for the family, it was challenging enough to start with standing on my front doorstep for a while. As this got easier to achieve and I could do it daily, I progressed to walking to the end of my drive and back on my own. The next step was to turn left and walk to the first lamp post. I would practise each progression until it felt doable and then add the smallest next step I could manage.

Over weeks, months and years, I did this. The walking progressed to running to the next lamp post. The runs progressed to a complete lap of my village, then the next village. Then I challenged myself with the Blenheim five-mile run, which I completed by running half and walking half (there are a lot of hills!). The next year, my challenge was to run, no matter how slowly, the whole course. The year after, my challenge was to beat my time. As I progressed with physical movement, my mental resilience built. As I ran, I started to manage the negative chatter in my head. I began to reframe those thoughts into more positive ones. Over the years, exercise has taught me I can achieve many things if my head is in the game and my brain is bought into what I'm working towards. As my exercise and physical fitness increased, so did my mental and emotional wellbeing.

Introduction

It was hard doing it on my own, but I found my way and have since continued living by that framework ever since. I explored my options for a framework and found the ones that resonated with me. It is important to note that all the methods and changes I tried and moved on from can and do work for others. Just not for me, not at that time of my life. This is why it is so important not to be influenced by whatever "new thing" is being marketed at you. It is why it is so important to do your own research, your own due diligence and find the way that works for you.

Again, I will state, I am not here to tell you what you need to do to help you SOS your life and live your Best Life. What I can show you is my flexible RoadMap to help you explore who you want to be and what you want to do. It is your responsibility to choose and action your change for your best life.

I have spent years helping others live better lives using this BestLife RoadMap. All those years of The Southey Way helping people live better lives has only confirmed the absolute uncompromising need for each of us to put ourselves first as individuals and find the way that works for each of us individually so we can live our best lives and be in the best health to help others in whatever our purpose is.

Is This Book for You?

Part of my BestLife RoadMap is being brutally honest with yourself. Before we get stuck in, it is important to check that this book is for you and that you are ready for this book.

This book is for you if you are one, some or all of the following:

- A purpose-led individual giving to everyone but yourself
- Committed to making change happen in all aspects of your life
- Missing having your life your way
- Believe you are worth investing in
- This book is not for you if you:
- Are genuinely happy with your whole life
- Are not ready to take responsibility for your life
- Don't take action on your "aha" moments
- Are not prepared to do different to get different
- Feel coaching and mentoring is not worth your time or investment

Introduction

What Can You Expect From This Book?

This book will give you the framework and skills to:

- Explore what your BestLife looks like and why
- Facilitate time for you to create your own bespoke BestLife RoadMap
- Continue living your BestLife Roadmap throughout your life journey
- Sustainably keep momentum on your BestLife RoadMap journey in all aspects

How Does The SOS BestLife RoadMap Work?

This book is a journey of five parts designed to be worked through, with you being the designer of your own BestLife RoadMap. Working from start to finish, this book will give you your personal and individual plan for your BestLife and many tools for managing the roadblocks and curveballs of life.

Once you have worked through each of the parts and found your current BestLife plan for A to Z, you can reuse the RoadMap tools regularly to keep reviewing and resetting as you move along your journey. Check in on your direction as life evolves. Being your own guide – being open to both internal and external observations, feeling, learning, changing and growing – can be hugely challenging, but also hugely rewarding and empowering.

Before we start this process together, please be super aware that work done on yourself at this personal level can make you feel very vulnerable and fearful. It can be challenging and scary. It can also be rewarding, empowering and life-changing in the best possible way!

If you come across any traumatic roadblocks along the way, please reach out for professional help. This book is designed as a guided self-help resource and should not be used as a substitute for therapy or medical advice. I would encourage you to reach out to relevant organisations if the need arises.

There are two facts of life: You are born (A) and you die (Z). The bit in the middle is life.

How you live your BestLife is up to you.

Are you ready to start?

Then let's get stuck in!

Part 1:

GroundWork A to Now

GroundWork: The A to Z Map of Your World

First, we need to clarify your starting point. Where are you now?

Without this reference point, you will not know where you currently are on your Map. Your life is your journey, and, as with all journeys, you must know your starting point before you can find your way to your destination. You need to know where you are leaving from and where you are heading so that you can create your journey's RoadMap.

So, let's set your starting point. From there, we will be able to look backwards and forwards along your journey and see whether you are still going in the right direction or are veering from the path you have chosen.

When you feel like making changes to your life, there is generally a reason to do so. Whether you're burning out, not spending enough time on a particular area of your life, a huge change is being forced upon you through illness or family, or simply a lack of time and energy for all the fun stuff. Or a hundred and one other reasons.

Before we go into where you are now, you need to be aware that living your life your way is not always as easy or logical as you think. You are being guided by an internal force, whether you like it or not!

Often, we don't know what it is specifically that we want to change. We just know something has got to!

Our brain will often hide from us the real reasons we want something different. This is because it is complex and has drives that we are not aware of, which keep us safe and functioning. This can impact your ability to take action on something you want to change. For example, if the change is too great, your brain will feel threatened and take action into play to keep you in the same place. Actions such as procrastination, impostor syndrome, anxiety or guilt could all be aspects of your brain keeping you where you are.

We have to do some investigative work to establish where we are now, so we know where we aim to get to. The more you know where your brain is at the starting point of your next journey, the more you can work with it to achieve what you want and travel down your new road to your BestLife. If your brain is aligned with your choices and it feels safe, then you will find the new route so much easier to plan and travel. If you don't align your brain with your heart and soul, the road can be unnecessarily challenging. Sounds like a lot less fun when we do things the hard way, right?

It is time to explore what is going on inside your body and mind. Learn how to help them work for you and not against you!

Brains and Thinking

First, it is helpful to understand a little about the brain and how it works and drives our actions. You don't need to be an expert, but it is important to know how our brains are made up and how they affect the way we live.

Brains and Evolution (the Reptilian Brain)

Neuroscientist Paul MacLean proposed the "Triune Brain" model in the 1960s, which suggests that the human brain is made up of three layers that emerged in succession during evolution:

The **Reptilian** brain, which is the oldest layer, controls basic vital functions like breathing, heart rate and physical balance. It's also known as the primal brain.

The **Limbic** brain, or the middle layer, controls emotional responses associated with emotions and value judgments. It develops based on instinct and past experiences.

The **Neocortex/Cerebral Cortex**, the outermost layer, controls language and reason. Generates higher cognitive functions like reasoning and logical thought.

Clear as mud? I know!

That is about as science-y as I will get, don't worry. If you are interested in learning more, there are many resources out there for you to lose yourself down that rabbit hole! The main point I want you to be aware of is the reptilian brain. It's a tricksy blighter!

You can be living your life, doing what you have always done, ticking the boxes of supposed success for your upbringing, relationships, community, etc., but not feeling fulfilled or particularly happy or unhappy. Neither do you feel especially driven to make a change to be happier or more fulfilled. You are simply not achieving what you want to, despite all your logical planning and goals.

GroundWork: The A to Z Map of Your World

Procrastination, distraction, a lack of motivation – they all keep you where you currently are. This is your reptilian brain keeping you in a box. It can be quite a comfortable box, but it is a box nonetheless. The box you are in represents success for the reptilian brain.

Remember, the reptilian brain is responsible for basic survival functions:

- ★ Control of survival activities (breathing, heart rate, balance and body temperature)
- ★ Simple actions (alertness, eating and basic procreation)
- ★ Fixed routines (lacking flexibility and emotion)
- ★ Innate behaviours (self-preservation, family preservation and reproduction)
- ★ Threat detection (distinguishing between threatening and non-threatening stimuli)
- ★ Fight or flight response (responding to threats with flight, fight or freeze)

The reptilian brain doesn't care if you are happy or sad, if you are having fun or are miserable, are living your best life or keeping on plodding on. If what you are currently doing hasn't killed you yet, then the reptilian brain will keep you doing what you have always done.

You are in your safe box.

You are not dead, so how you are living is clearly successful.

As far as the reptilian brain is concerned, you are winning at life because you are alive.

Do you feel like you are winning, though? Is this the criteria for your thriving life?

Doesn't sound like much fun to me.

And as we only have one go on this journey from A to Z (and we are hopefully not being chased by a lion), there is clearly more to life than the reptilian brain's safety box! This brings me to the second brain area to have some understanding around.

How We Think (Or Don't Think!)

Without an awareness of what is happening when you think and how much goes on in your brain that you are not in control of, you cannot align your decisions with actions that will reassure your reptilian brain and reprogram

GroundWork: The A to Z Map of Your World

your default settings. In brief, your brain works on three levels of consciousness: the conscious, subconscious and unconscious. All contribute to how you think and behave.

Conscious mind. This is what we are aware of at any given moment, including our thoughts, actions and perceptions. Thinking, working something out, learning or doing something new all reside in our conscious mind.

Subconscious mind. This is where automatic reactions and actions take place, such as driving a car. We can become aware of these actions if we think about them. Your default settings and habitual behaviour live here.

Unconscious mind. This is where our memories and events are stored, including thoughts and desires buried deep within us. These memories and experiences shape our beliefs, habits and behaviours. For example: "Last time I did this, it made me nervous, so I'll be wary next time," or "When I did this, it hurt, so I'll not do it again." How to stay alive and lessons learned live here.

There is a growing awareness of the importance of these levels of consciousness, especially with regard to our mental health. It is good to clarify the differences between the three, as there can be confusion when we are talking about how to make changes to our lives.

The jury is out on where exactly all the evolutionary brain layers and aspects involved sit within the mind. The brain is a supercomplex organ; it is most definitely not straightforward. Scientists are still exploring and discovering the power the brain has, but we as individuals don't need to know more than these simple facts on the day-to-day:

The reptilian brain keeps you safe and alive. Working with your unconscious mind, it has learned that what didn't harm you before must be safe. So it's perfectly content for you to keep doing the same things, simply because they didn't kill you. It has zero interest in how happy or fulfilling you find your life. All changing behaviour is measured against the criteria of "Is it too risky?" Or "Will it cause harm or even kill us?"

Your conscious mind is the change maker. It is aware of emotions and feelings and has a logical approach to decision-making and implementing changes within your life. All decisions made by the conscious mind must reassure the unconscious mind and reptilian brain that it is for the greater good, for survival and worth any perceived risk. In other words, to create an action, the rewards must be greater than the risks to the reptilian brain. It is the job of your conscious mind to build that case *for* change and make it irresistible; to make it so that inaction is a risk in itself.

GroundWork: The A to Z Map of Your World

Your subconscious mind is there to take the load off. After you have built a strong case for change in your conscious mind and have reassured your unconscious mind, then you need to practise the steps to make this habitual. This is the superpower of your subconscious mind. It is like a computer (ie, when this happens, then that happens). A default setting if you like, and one you get to choose and create with your conscious mind and repetition!

In summary, what you can see from this snapshot is that the tricksy reptilian brain is fast, automatic and impulsive. It seeks out activities that are safe and don't require much thought. When activated, the reptilian brain can cause a person to express emotions like fear, anger, shame, guilt and grief and take actions without thought to what we consciously want to achieve, say or do!

But when you align all three consciousnesses, your success rate for creating, actioning and sustaining change in your life increases. You get to live the life you choose and not the reptilian default setting of staying in your box, counting simply being alive as success!

Where does your life measure right now?

Now you know the basics of your internal guiding forces, let's have a look at the common aspects involved in the lives of humans and their importance. With this knowledge, you will then be able to measure where you sit within these parameters of your own life. After all, if you don't know what you're measuring, you will never know where you are.

Your Best Health

Your health is vital to your BestLife, but is often left to the end of the list. To understand what a thriving life looks like, you have to see thriving alongside the other two important life levels of surviving and belonging. Let's explore the 3 Levels of Living.

Surviving

To survive, humans need the following basic needs:

- ★ **Food.** The body needs calories and nutrients to grow, function and repair.

- ★ **Water.** The body needs water to process food and remove waste.

- ★ **Air.** Humans need air to breathe.

- ★ **Shelter.** Humans need protection from the elements.

GroundWork: The A to Z Map of Your World

- ★ **Sleep.** Humans need sleep to learn new things and get past emotional pain.

The language is really important here. This is to survive. The more we do, the more we're going to survive, the better we're going to survive. There is no point in faffing about with trendy magic supplements or the next new, amazing thing if you are not nailing these basics.

Did you notice exercise isn't even on here? You don't have to do heavy exercises daily; there's no need for 10,000 steps every day. This is survival, so these needs are foundational. The more you maximise these, the stronger the foundations you have for life and the more you can build your BestLife without it feeling fragile and wobbly!

Belonging

In addition to these basic needs, humans also have needs for belonging and becoming.

- ★ **Belonging.** Humans need to connect with others and feel like part of a community.

- ★ **Becoming.** Humans need to grow and develop as individuals and reach their full potential.

Your connection with other people and how you are sharing your energy with others can either feed your soul or drain you dry. As humans, we need that connection with other people, of being part of a community. We are not an island of one person. If you are an introvert, you still need people. There's got to be some kind of interaction in there, and the ability to learn, grow and develop. Choose your interactions wisely. Communication and understanding are the foundations of every relationship. And even when there are disagreements, open communication and listening to hear what is said, with the intent of understanding, leaves us better off than judgemental behaviour. Worse would be having someone force their opinion on us.

Learning about what is driving you, what you love to do and then finding communities that will enable you to learn and grow will fill the human needs of connection, community and learning. And don't forget to be a good listener and keep an open mind about other ways of thinking and community.

Thriving

On top of these, nowadays humans have needs to fulfil that spread far and wide beyond our own selves:

- ★ Family
- ★ Friends
- ★ Work
- ★ Community
- ★ The world

This can be classed as the giving back stage, because this is what elevates us. But you've got to choose how you do it. So if it's taking away from your basic needs to do this, you're making your foundations crumble. If you focus too much here before you have your basic and thriving needs developed, you may find yourself giving and giving without any returns. Your foundations may start to wobble and you may feel out of control and vulnerable. When you give too much without filling up on your basic and thriving needs, you will run out of energy quickly and end up, like I did, physically unable to function.

So once you are confident that your basic and thriving needs are being consistently and sustainably maintained at a level you need, then it is time to look into the higher needs of purpose and giving back.

The connections that truly uplift us are those that bring a sense of wellbeing, not obligation. With obligation comes the feeling of other people's expectations weighing down on us. The feeling of giving voluntarily turns into a feeling of having something taken from us. When others choose your actions, you can feel taken advantage of. When you choose your actions, you feel empowered.

Developing your 3 Levels of Living can help you stay mentally healthy and feeling good. It also helps you live longer and have more fun. On the flipside, you may feel increased anxiety and overwhelm when you are not meeting those needs in accordance with what your brain expects.

To survive is what your reptilian brain requires above and beyond anything else. The quicker and more consistently you solidify those basic needs, the better. To thrive, we need to know, learn, practise and live all these aspects of life, in relation to their importance to us as individuals.

Seems huge, right? Already feeling a little overwhelmed?

You're likely already busy and frustrated, feeling not as happy as you want or could be. And now, I'm showing you

GroundWork: The A to Z Map of Your World

loads more things you probably hadn't even thought about putting on your very long to-do list.

Don't panic!

Remember, this section of the book is all about where you are now. It's about taking your life out of the reptilian safe box and having a good look at it. I promise that I will give you an easy straightforward method of sorting and organising all the shit in your life, getting rid of what doesn't serve you and putting the items you want to keep back into your life in an actionable and sustainable way.

If you have faith in my process, clarity, fun and freedom will rule. You will end up with a clear picture of where you are so that you have space to decide where you want to go next!

The following exercise will help you take all the aspects of your current life out of your head and onto paper, where you will be able to see it for what it is. If you are not aware of it, you cannot change it. And whilst it is all crammed into your busy brain, there is no space for you to see it to sort it out.

We will explore together how you will sort through and decide what goes back in and what you will leave out.

Exercise: Brain Dump Mind Map

The purpose of this exercise is to establish where your time goes and what you do currently in your life. Most people are not aware of exactly how much they do until it is written down in front of them. This exercise is designed to bring your awareness to how much you *actually* do in your life.

A mind map is a powerful process that allows you to explore and organise your thoughts in a structured but creative way, allowing you to visualise and develop a topic. In other words, it is a process that frees you from overthinking everything around a topic and allows your unconscious mind to have a say in what is going on.

So let's begin.

On a large clean piece of paper, draw a smiley face right in the middle, about the size of a 50p piece. This represents you.

Around your smiling face, write the main categories of your life. If you are not sure, use the survival, basic and life needs list from the previous section as prompts. Remember, this is about *your* life and what it all means to you. There are no right or wrong answers. Write the important categories

GroundWork: The A to Z Map of Your World

down, whatever they are. If they are important to you, they need to be on paper. For example: Work, Partner, Kids, Pets, Home, Family, Friends, Community etc.

The next step is to brain dump all your tasks and jobs around each category you have made. List all the things you do in your life on a daily, weekly, monthly and yearly basis. Use your main categories as prompts. Add in anything that doesn't fit into the main categories, too. For example, if I were to take the category "home," I could put washing, cleaning, tidying, ironing, cooking, watching, meals, paying bills etc.

Do not overthink this process. I want everything there from visits to your parents, to school runs and your daily commute, your underwater basket-weaving classes and running errands for your neighbour. Everything!

Don't stop writing until your brain is empty. Then ask yourself, what else? And repeat.

If it helps, turn it into a game. Set a timer for five minutes and write as many as you can. Walk away, make a cuppa. Come back, set another timer for another five minutes and go again.

Do whatever works for you to empty your brain onto this paper, everything you do.

When you have finished, you will probably have quite a messy-looking brain dump in front of you.

Do *not* tidy it up!

Put this sheet to one side. We will come back to it later when we start creating your Route to your BestLife.

Bonus Time

Write down the emotions and feelings you have experienced. Write anything. There are no rights or wrongs.

How do you feel after this exercise?

What have you learned about yourself by doing this exercise?

A to Now: Are You Currently Thriving?

In the previous section, we looked at where you are now with regard to what you are *doing* on a day-to-day basis. This is important to know and record because it is where your time and energy are currently going from a task perspective. Very practical as you spend most of your life doing!

However, humans are emotional beings and therefore driven by those emotions. So, whether you are happy with your status quo or not will affect how you feel and whether you feel like you are thriving and living your best life or just surviving. It's time to examine what a thriving best life actually entails and where you currently stand on the scale of 1 to 10.

Are you at survival level and barely holding your head above water (Level 1)? Are you at Level 10? Life is tickety-boo and couldn't be better! Or are you somewhere in between? To start, let's quickly recap those 3 Levels of Living.

Surviving (Basic Needs)

- ★ **Food.** The body needs calories and nutrients to grow, function and repair.

- ★ **Water.** The body needs water to process food and remove waste.

- ★ **Air.** Humans need air to breathe.

- ★ **Shelter.** Humans need protection from the elements.

- ★ **Sleep.** Humans need sleep to learn new things and get past emotional pain.

Belonging
(Needs for Belonging and Becoming)

- ★ **Belonging.** Humans need to connect with others and feel like they are part of a community.

- ★ **Becoming.** Humans need to grow and develop as individuals and reach their full potential.

A to Now: Are You Currently Thriving?

Thriving (Needs That Spread Past Ourselves)

★ Family

★ Friends

★ Work

★ Community

★ Social responsibilities

★ The world

★ Etc.

In the last section, we explored the need to have all three levels fulfilled for life to be thriving. It is important to remember that it must work for you. These three levels are generic needs, so defining what they mean to you requires deciding how you'll measure the extent to which you're thriving.

Life can become comfortable and routine. You achieve a certain level, status, skill set, success etc, and settle into your life. Your current state of affairs could seem perfectly satisfactory on the surface. But if you scratch that surface and do some exploratory work, you may find areas of your life that are not quite what they seem, or quite what you want them to be.

Routine can be great if we have chosen it and we continue to actively choose it.

However, routine can be the start of a slippery slope to complacency, which can drift into mediocrity and behaviours that you perhaps don't actively choose for yourself. If you don't check regularly, you may not realise that life could be lived in a better way for you.

This exact thing happened to me.

My husband and I moved to New Jersey in 1999 for his job. Our visas didn't allow me to work, so I paused my salaried career. At this point, I started my voluntary job of raising my children. We moved back to the UK in 2003 with a 3-month-old and a 2-year-old after 5 years away. Once we settled in our new home, we made the decision together that I would stay home and raise the children. For most of the 2000s, I was at home full-time bringing up my young kids whilst hubby travelled for work and came home on the weekends.

I thought I was doing OK.

My checklist measures of success day to day were:

- Are the kids happy?

A to Now: Are You Currently Thriving?

- Did they eat well, get bathed regularly and sleep well?

- Did they get to school, have their play dates?

- Did the dog get its daily walk?

- Is there food in the house for the weekend?

- Did the house get its regular cleaning?

- Does everybody have enough clean pants and socks?

I ticked all the boxes, daily, regularly, for several years. And because I was ticking the boxes, I thought all was well and good. And on the outside, to everyone else, it was. I looked like I was thriving. I even thought this was as good as life got. I mean, sounds like the dream life, right? So much fun!

For the first five years after our return from America, I was so focused on doing a good job raising our kids and supporting my husband that I was completely unaware I had planned my whole life around the hubby and the kids. It wasn't until 2006, when the kids were in primary school, that I realised I did absolutely nothing for myself. I had no identity outside of being a wife and mother. I had no drive to expand my world or my life outside of the house. I had no energy left to do anything. I didn't share with anyone how I felt, as it seemed like admitting failure in the role that I had chosen.

I rarely went out, and when I did, it was like another person was being released. Drinking and partying with no off switch. I was known for being the last to leave any party and could throw a tantrum if I was asked to leave before it was fully over!

Two extremes: one super responsible and one completely irresponsible. And I had no idea who either of these two people was. On the one hand, for the most part, I was being super sensible, grown up and doing everything "right," and on the other, playing like a big kid just let out of detention! There was no middle ground behaviour.

Self-care and self-awareness weren't a thing in my world then. If you looked like you were coping, then all was well. You know the phrase, "Keep on carrying on"? That was exactly what I did. To the detriment of my own happiness. I considered myself living successfully as long as I was able to maintain the illusion and nobody realised how much of a failure I was.

I was miserable, but feeling guilty about being miserable. Clearly, I had all that the UK culture told me I was meant

A to Now: Are You Currently Thriving?

to value in life: a brilliant husband, two gorgeous kids, a lovely home and enough money to not worry about the day to day. I should be happy and grateful, especially when so many people have so much less.

When life is challenging, there's often a moment that makes you realise things can't stay the way they are. A moment in time. A fork in the road that forces you to make a decision. I'm so stubborn that it took three "The Moments" before I got the message!

The first was the thought I had whilst driving to the supermarket.

The kids were at school, my husband was at work and I was doing the chores. Driving down the dual carriageway towards the shops, I remember, clear as day, thinking "I wonder if anyone would notice if I just drove off the road into the bridge." I didn't do it. I just kept on carrying on.

This was shortly followed by moment number two at a family birthday party. I felt like I wasn't present at all, simply watching from above as my family, friends and I enjoyed ourselves at the party. Looking at the pictures afterwards, I didn't recognise the happy-looking Sara. It felt like a lie.

I hadn't realised how bad it had got until moment number three: a routine GP visit where I struggled not to sob and fall apart when I was asked if I was OK.

I realised then that I wasn't okay. I wasn't living. I was, in fact, barely surviving. Living wasn't meant to be ticking the boxes for everyone else to be happy and OK. Living well was not a case of hiding so that nobody noticed I was miserable.

The result of my breakdown was that the GP pronounced me as suffering from severe depression. It was a relief to know I wasn't actually failing at life, that I wasn't a bad mother or person. There was a reason!

All the time I had been coping and ticking my boxes, I thought I was doing the right thing by putting everyone first. In fact, what I had done was put myself last, consistently, for years! It wasn't until that healthcare visit that I realised this.

It was a huge relief to know that I had lost my way. Because once I knew that, I knew I could find my way back to me, to my path, to my life.

I had been living in a maze within a box with the lid shut tight. I'd been following an invisible path that I didn't

A to Now: Are You Currently Thriving?

choose, and bashing my head against the walls holding me in.

I hadn't been thriving. I had been surviving.

I didn't even know who I was any more.

The box I had been in had gotten so full, airless and small that there was no room for me to flourish, to grow vigorously or otherwise!

I was most definitely stuck at Level 1 of the 3 Levels of Living, and I hadn't even realised! As soon as that lid got unstuck and I saw a glimmer of life outside the box, I hadn't realised how much I was not thriving, how much I wasn't living life.

I realised then that something had to change. The lid needed to be lifted. A thorough examination of the contents of my box was necessary, and decisions needed to be made. I had not realised how stuck in survival I was until I was forced to stop, take a breath and look at myself and my life.

From this moment on, in 2006 and forever moving forward, I have been doing just that. I regularly take the opportunity to stop, breathe and review how I am and whether I am on the right path for thriving, not just surviving. By doing this regularly, I can catch any deviations before they take me too far away from the road of my choosing. No more getting lost accidentally!

My purpose in sharing this story is to show you how easy it is to live in a way that feels like thriving, but is actually just surviving. When you can recognise when you are simply surviving and not thriving, you then have an opportunity to change course. If you don't know and you don't give yourself a chance to find out, then you'll continue not to live the best life you could.

What could you be missing out on by staying tightly locked into that survival box? What does living your life in the box actually look like?

It could be restricting your activities or hobbies because of work commitments. Or giving your free time to others instead of ring-fencing time to yourself. It could be saying "yes" to things you don't want to do and "no" to things you do want to do.

What does lifting the lid on your box look like?

Seeing the possibilities available and having a choice. Being able to choose actions that are in alignment with

A to Now: Are You Currently Thriving?

where you want to go and how you want to live. Having boundaries around activities that are essential to you. Looking at possibilities with an open mind and dreaming of where they could take you. Deciding to do something different just because you want to. To be in your own power and opportunity.

The purpose of this next exercise is exactly this: Allow yourself time to find out what your in and out of the box looks like. Find out what surviving vs. thriving looks like for you, because once you are aware of this, you can make changes.

You can use this same process to regularly review and work on your life *while* living your BestLife. You can keep the lid on your box loose and liftable, allowing you to see your exciting path. Never get stuck in your box with no room to thrive, so that you are always in a position to choose your own path.

The aim is for free-range living! Choose whatever direction works for you.

Exercise: In and Out of the Box

This exercise will help you see where you currently are and how you are living your life. It can show you areas of your life that are holding you back and keeping you contained in your box. Think of it like a satisfaction survey. Check in with all the things you do, where you spend your time and how happy that currently makes you. Answer the following questions in relation to your life as it is right now. Separate the questions according to your current box, what's outside it, and the 3 Levels of Living.

Do not overthink your answers. A few quick words will tell you more than a well-planned essay. Spend a maximum of 10 minutes on the whole process. You can either speak, draw, write or even make a mind map of your answers to the questions below. Be honest with yourself about the current state of your box! Look at your answers to previous exercises, as well as anything else that pops out of your current life box.

Your Current Box

What is great about your life?

What is not so great?

How do you feel most of the time?

Who brings you the most happiness?

A to Now: Are You Currently Thriving?

What makes you laugh?

What makes you sad?

Where are you most satisfied?

Where are you most unhappy?

What is stopping you from making changes?

Out of Your Box

What could you change?

Why would you change your life?

Who needs to be more in or more out of your life?

What is missing?

What don't you currently do that you would like to do?

3 Levels of Living

Where are you currently on the three 3 Levels of Living?

How could you move yourself up a level or partial level closer to thriving?

What or who is pulling you down a level closer to survival?

Bonus Time

If you feel you would like to explore more, use the strong question words below to ask yourself even more about your life. The words are there so you can ask yourself open questions. Note that yes-or-no answers will not give you a great picture of where you currently are.

Who...? Why...? What...? Where...? When...? How...?

We will come back to your answers further on in the book. However, you will already see and feel some areas you are more aware of that you can look to improve. Hopefully, you have also seen some wonderful areas you are happy with, wouldn't change, and you can recognise and value in your life. This is the start of your process for creating your BestLife RoadMap route plan. And as with all plans, you choose what you are going to action. It may feel overwhelming if you have a lot you'd like to change. Remember that it is the reptilian brain at work, keeping you safe.

Don't panic! The first step is to look and become aware. Then we can choose and change!

Who Are You?

Now that you have opened the box of your current life and given it a good airing, you can take a close, honest look at yourself and who you are. To sustainably and consistently live your BestLife, it is helpful to discover who you are, what you want out of life and what drives you forward. Once you know who you are, it is also helpful to check in with that "who" on a regular basis to ensure you are still being true to your "who"! You have probably never been taught how to discover who you are and what is important to you.

The accepted way is to learn by example from your parents and family, as well as from school and the people around you as you work and grow up. Essentially, most of your thoughts and opinions are developed from outside influences. There isn't a "Life Skills" curriculum at school, nor a space to explore your inner thoughts and workings whilst you complete university or college. By the time you are working for a living, chances are you are too busy to stop and analyse why it is you believe or support a particular thing (e.g. opinions, political parties or religion).

You may have grown up in a family whose values conflicted with your own, causing stress and anxiety, or sometimes even behaviour you wouldn't have chosen otherwise. Then there are also times you're put on the spot and challenged by someone with opposing views, forcing you to defend something you believe in.

If you have not had the opportunity to look within yourself and discover what is important to you on a fundamental level, it can leave you feeling out of control on your journey through life. When you're unclear about your own values, you're likely to live by those of the people around you – not because you choose to, but because it's easier to go with the flow than to take a different path. What drives you forward, keeps you on your path and helps you thrive in life are your core values.

Your Core Values

Core values are part of your internal guide. They steer you either consciously or subconsciously through the twists and turns of life. There is no compromise when it comes to core values; they are your moral compass and the measure of everything you do.

So, what are core values?

You may have come across this concept within the business world or, if you run your own business, you've likely done work on this. Think of the mission statements and company values you typically see within office buildings and on marketing materials.

Your core values as an individual are the fundamental beliefs and ethics that guide your actions, behaviours and decision-making. They help define you as a person. They create a solid foundation for your vision of life, for how and what you focus on.

Core values are anything you feel super strongly about.

For example:

> Any lie is unacceptable, even the little white lies told to ease someone else's discomfort.
>
> Family always comes first, no matter what.
>
> Never hurt the ones you love.

Core values often, but not always, stay with you for a lifetime. They typically derive from our upbringing, from our family and from those early experiences of life.

Some of my lifelong core values:

> Always hug the ones you love and tell them you love them often.
>
> Never leave someone worse off than when you found them.
>
> See the positive in everyone.
>
> Expect the best, plan for the worst.
>
> Never underestimate the impact you have on others.

These are the lasting core principles I have aimed to live by in good, bad and ugly times. You can choose to lose or change them over time, as you travel along this road called life. If you were raised with a core value that no longer serves you as you become more independent, it can be helpful to consider whether you want to let it go completely or adapt it to better support the life you're creating.

For example, here are a few core values I grew up with that I have decided to adapt or lose:

Always save for a rainy day. My personal belief now is that every day is for living to the full, not waiting for it all to go awry.

You can't enjoy it unless you've earned it. I now believe there is enjoyment in all aspects of life, whether you earned it or not.

Work hard so you can retire well. I believe in living well within the moment each and every day, doing what I love for as long as I can.

From my experience with my family's core beliefs, I've learned a few new ones:

Live in the moment, not the past or the future.

Live by my agenda and not anybody else's.

You cannot please all the people all of the time, but you can withdraw gracefully.

Without examining both past and present core values, understanding what your personal values mean to you and how they shape your life, you can't create a sustainable, consistent RoadMap for your future.

When you live in alignment with your values, you will be living in alignment with your BestLife. If you live out of alignment with your values, you will probably find life more challenging than it needs to be.

For example, if one of your core values is to always tell the truth, but your work requires you to regularly bend the truth, that wouldn't lead to a happy life. Your job would be in direct conflict with your core value. Now, if you believe in following the law to the letter, working in the police force would allow your values to be in alignment with your job, leading to a better chance of happiness.

Every time you check in with your core values and what you believe to be true, you have an incredible opportunity to strengthen your ability to live your best life. It is an opportunity to cement your commitment to yourself and your path moving forward. You strengthen your decision to live your life your way and not anybody else's way.

Some core values remain with us for a long time, but some can serve a purpose at a particular time in our lives. This is often influenced by our upbringing, the people around us and the stage of life we're in, among other factors. Knowing your core values and why you choose them can help guide you to living your best life.

Examples of short-term core values:

> I choose to work hard for three years so I can take a year off to travel.
>
> Success is a nice house and a shiny new car.
>
> Success is a home big enough for my extended family.
>
> Success is a hut by the sea with my dog.
>
> My value within the family unit is not dependent on how much money I earn.

Core values you don't actively choose and are forced to live by can be quite damaging to your ability to thrive. It is important to look at your life values and see where they come from and whether they truly are serving you.

Identifying the values you currently live by that do not serve you can be a game-changer. Figure out why they aren't working for you and decide how to reframe them. Or you can kick them out of your life altogether!

Here are a few of mine that I ditched because they didn't serve my best life:

> Being available 24/7 to my kids will give them the best chance of being well-balanced humans.

If I say yes to everything, everyone will like me.

If I disagree with people, they will hate me.

I must always respect my elders.

Do what society expects of you.

I have replaced these values with the following:

Setting boundaries and expectations frees me to be my true self and helps me help others more.

Saying no to actions I don't want to do frees me up to say yes to the actions that fill my soul.

I am not for everyone and not everyone is for me. That is totally OK.

I am solely responsible for my own actions and reactions, and I get to choose them.

Always question why when the word "should" is used.

And my all-time favourite that I use daily:

Adulting is overrated – only do it when you have to!

Your Purpose

Your core values can also be guided by your purpose, and your purpose can be guided by your core values. Either way, it's helpful to reflect on what purpose means: what it means to you, to your best life and how it can influence the choices you make as you move forward on your life's journey.

If you were lucky, you knew early on what you'd like to be as an adult. If you were exceptionally lucky, you kept that wish and actually got to do it. As is more likely though, you didn't have a clue, or you haven't been able to fulfil that dream your young self once had. Being asked this as a kid in school may have been super frustrating if you didn't have an answer; almost like you've failed before you've even started at "proper" life!

Fear not!

I like to think of your purpose as something that aligns with your core values. It isn't always as obvious as knowing what you want to be when you grow up! So long as you live life being honest with yourself about what makes you happy and what doesn't, then your road will lead you to your purpose. You will enjoy the journey along the way.

There is a lot of talk about a purpose-led life. It starts when you are a child and never seems to stop. If you are lucky enough to discover your purpose early on, it can steer you well, so long as you keep checking that it is still in alignment with your core and life values.

If you don't know what your purpose in life is or haven't found the thing that floats your boat and lights up your soul, take heart. If you work on your best life, you will. The beauty about the BestLife RoadMap is that you can still live your best life whilst figuring it out! You will not miss out or feel deprived because you are choosing what makes you happy all the way through.

Here's my story about not having a purpose and how it affected my life.

I was that kid in secondary school who did not know what I wanted to be. I remember being asked this in primary school in the 80s. I responded very confidently that I wanted to be a fighter pilot because my father was one. I grew up on an RAF camp being woken by the Red Arrows at the crack of dawn! A classic case of other people's values influencing my own. When I asked, I was told in no uncertain terms that girls weren't allowed. By the time women were allowed to fly fighters, my eyesight was too bad, so that disqualified me again. I was offered a career path in air traffic control instead, which essentially meant watching and guiding all those lucky people doing what I would have loved to do. No, thank you!

I spent many years in various jobs trying to find something that floated my boat. You read my potted history at the beginning of this book. A core value I carried through this period was to find the good in each job and leave before a sad one took my soul.

My path has taken me to many places and roles, including secretarial, administrative, accounting, recruitment, account management, project management, corporate training in IT and people management, Human Resources, gardening and garden design, as well as child-rearing.

I am trained and qualified in a lot of industries.

Most of my jobs involved working closely with others, which helped me fulfil one of my core values. But I still didn't have a purpose.

As I mentioned previously, it wasn't until 2016 that I discovered my purpose: helping individuals thrive. But I wouldn't have found it without travelling all the previous roads, through the many jobs and industries I worked in along the way.

The multitude of different experiences gave me the skills and confidence to realise my purpose after my 10 years of darkness. Without them, I wouldn't have known when my moment of purpose revealed itself. I am on a mission to help the world thrive, one individual at a time. If you are thriving, then you are better able to help others. And those others will be better able to help their people. And so the map of roads fans out!

If you think in small steps, it is possible to keep living your best life whilst moving towards a purpose now or in the future. By knowing and living your core values, you can enjoy the journey, whether you have yet to discover your purpose or not.

So, what roads are you going to take to find your core values and live your purpose? Thus far, we have explored why core values and purpose are so useful in living your best life. But how do you determine what they are?

Because they are essentially beliefs that are held at the core of our beings, they can often be tricky to identify. Often, we are guided by them without even being aware of them!

There are several ways to dig deep and discover your core values. One of the easiest ways to start is by examining situations or events in your life that have caused you to experience strong emotions. Times when you feel like you "should" do something but you don't want to, moments when someone pushes your buttons and you get angry. Examining these situations after they have occurred can shed light on what we are feeling. Then you can ask yourself why you're feeling that way, and whether you want to keep feeling it.

I will give you one of my examples.

An unspoken rule in the UK is never to discuss politics or religion at the dinner table because it can be so emotive. People have very strong opinions and beliefs about both topics, and will usually not even consider others.

I grew up in a multi-generational household. My brother and I, my parents, my mother's parents and my great-grandmother all lived in the same house. Out of all of us, most were ardent socialists, half were Catholic, half Church of England, all opinionated and not afraid to share those opinions. Dinner times were always noisy, always full of debate and opinion, with emotions running high. This was my normal. One of their values was to always fight for those not able to fight for themselves. Opinions would differ as to who those people were and who was at fault for their suffering. You had to have a strong opinion and voice to be able to stand your ground, or even get a word in.

Although I loved living in our large family, I was less a fan of the debates and how emotional they used to get. I have always been hugely sensitive to people's feelings, and I would absorb them all as debates raged around the table. Very early on, I developed a huge dislike of conflict. When I opened my mouth to say something, I often felt shouted over or told I was wrong. It always seemed that I was the only one not able to express my opinion in a way that would be heard. So, I learned to keep my opinions to myself. If I didn't share them, nobody could tell me I was wrong! I found the whole experience emotionally upsetting and even traumatic, and I began to actively avoid any situation where conflict might arise.

This belief has stayed with me throughout my life, until a family meal in 2024, when I stated my political preference and added my boundaries: I will share and engage in debates now, but I will actively withdraw from conversations when they become too overwhelming.

From this story, I can deduce that I have core values around:

Emotional and mental health. I put my emotional and mental wellbeing first and will not sacrifice it to fit in.

Belief in myself. My worth is not given to me by anybody else but me.

Conflict. Debate is good when done in a respectful, inclusive and open-minded manner and boundaries are heeded.

I would highly recommend you spend time hunting out your core values. Find out what matters to you!

Here are a few questions to help you ferret them out and write them down.

If you need some prompting on your current life core values, review your work on the previous exercises, watch and read the news, replay discussions with family and friends, and more. See what evokes an emotion or memory in you that feels strong and has you passionately agreeing or disagreeing with it. Then ask yourself why you feel that way.

Topics that can be explored include:

- ★ Right and wrong in specific contexts like relationships, community, country etc.
- ★ Topics you have to share your opinion on
- ★ Stuff that drives you crazy

- ★ Actions that make you angry
- ★ Actions and people that inspire or repel you
- ★ Ways you enjoy spending your time
- ★ How you would like to be treated and shown love and respect
- ★ Topics that cause you to get into arguments

Make a note of your key values so they are in your conscious mind. Having them in your conscious mind means you can check:

- ★ Your core values and purpose are still serving who you currently are.
- ★ Your path to your BestLife is in alignment with your core values.
- ★ For any changes and additions you want to make on a new route you may want to take.

If you don't know, you can't change. Making a note and checking in on your values will help you keep focused on your journey ahead.

Exercise: What is Important to You?

Use this opportunity to explore and write down values and points of purpose that matter to you. It is good to have them written down for you to check in with on a regular basis. By checking, you can ensure you still believe them to be true, whether they still serve you in your life and whether you are still moving forwards down your BestLife Road.

Take 10 minutes to write the answers to these questions. Again, don't think too hard. Your first answer is likely to be your truest in the moment!

What are the values you currently live by?

What drives you to get up every day and keep going?

Where do you modify your natural behaviour to conform to others' expectations?

What in your life makes you happy?

What guides you through this phase of your life?

What is your current purpose in life?

Where do people tell you you are brilliant?

Where do you create ripples or waves?

What is your meaning of life?

What values do you put on yourself?

Once you've completed this exercise, you will have an idea of who you are and what you value in life. It doesn't have to be fully formed. Bringing these questions into your conscious mind is a great starting point. These questions can be asked regularly and often. You may be surprised at how your answers evolve.

Bonus Time

If you are ready to, and only if you feel ready, write down your list of values and, if you have found it already, your purpose in life. Place it somewhere you see often. I have mine as a pinned note on my phone!

Don't be afraid to get creative if you are not a words-on-a-page person. For example, pictures can represent so much if they are dialled into your values.

My core values are:

My purpose is:

How Are You?

There is an area we haven't yet covered within this Groundwork: A - Z Map of Your World section. It is an essential part of living your best life: your health.

When I talk about health, I mean *all* aspects that affect it, whether emotional, mental, as well as physical. One cannot be totally separated from the others. All three are interlinked, and the results you get will depend on their interaction. If you are working under tight deadlines, the physical reaction is that you will feel tired and run down. Chances are you will also feel stressed, anxious or sad. You may struggle to get motivated to do anything, procrastinate and avoid essential tasks because the overwhelm is too great.

When you feel mentally challenged or emotionally wrung out, it is harder to get moving and carry out the basic physical health requirements that support your survival level. This can lead to your foundational groundwork becoming wobbly. To use a travel analogy, you start hitting the potholes because you don't notice them, rather than recognising and going around them or filling them in and smoothing the road out.

Your health is foundational. It is a requirement for you to survive at the very minimum. It is also often the first thing that falls by the wayside when life gets hard. The reason? Other demands shout louder than your own requirements. The consequences of failing external demands are more visible and far more painful than those of simply skipping a workout or eating your vegetables! Let's quickly take a look at the expectations for health as a population. The UK government health guidelines are as follows:

Exercise. Be active. Have at least 150 minutes of moderate intensity exercise per week (increased breathing and able to talk) or at least 75 minutes of vigorous intensity exercise per week (breathing fast and difficulty talking), or a combination of both. Minimise sedentary time by breaking up periods of inactivity.

Strength. Build strength at least two days a week.

Balance. For older individuals to reduce the chance of frailty and falls, improve balance 2 days a week.

Nutrition. The Eatwell Guide shows the proportions of the main food groups that form a healthy, balanced diet:

- ★ Eat at least five portions of a variety of fruit and vegetables every day

- ★ Base meals on potatoes, bread, rice, pasta and other starchy carbohydrates, choosing wholegrain versions where possible

- ★ Have some dairy or dairy alternatives (such as soy drinks); choose lower-fat and lower-sugar options

- ★ Regularly eat beans, pulses, fish, eggs, meat and other proteins (including two portions of fish every week, one of which should be oily)

- ★ Choose unsaturated oils and spreads and eat in small amounts

- ★ Drink six to eight glasses of fluid a day

If consuming foods and drinks high in fat, salt or sugar have these less often and in small amounts. Additionally, government guidelines recommend seven to nine hours of sleep per night. And that is all it said!

You can see that at best, the recommendations are general and high-level. At worst, they are woefully inadequate to help anyone looking to live their best life. Unless you have a clear idea of what it is you're looking for, trying to get a plan together for your best health, without using Dr. Google or a random webpage trying to sell some magical cure, will be near impossible. Without going into huge detail (enough content there for another, future book), here is my basic rundown on what areas you need to consider to increase your health.

3Y's: You, Your Essentials, Your Lifestyle

These 3Y's for your BestHealth break down a huge and complicated subject, one that brings in many billions of pounds of income for companies in the health and wellbeing industry. It is such an essential part of living that it can cause pain in your life when you haven't got it right. These companies prey on that pain. For the majority of these companies, getting you to spend your money on them, and keep on doing so, is far more important than your actual pain, needs and requirements.

If you take what you learn about yourself from this book and apply it logically and consistently, with responsibility and research (using your conscious mind), you'll make better decisions. When you're not acting out of pain, fear or desperation (driven by your tricksy reptilian brain), you'll be able to choose to spend your money where it benefits you most. I hope the following 3Y's will help you make the great choices for *you,* not for those ethically suspect companies!

I have split the topic BestHealth into the 3Y's: You, Your Essentials, Your Lifestyle. By splitting health up into these three categories, it will be easier for you to monitor how you are doing and where you want to concentrate your efforts and energy. As with the Levels of Life, the 3Ys work in conjunction with each other. The following is a brief explanation of my 3Ys, what they mean to you, your health and your BestLife and how you can use them to keep a close eye on any changes that you may need.

You

This is your bird's eye view of how you are doing in the following areas of your life: physical health, mental health, emotional health, confidence and happiness.

These five areas are the most commonly used signs of good health for individuals.

Physical Health

The condition of your physical body. Affected by lifestyle choices, genetics and physiology, environment and access to healthcare. Taking care of your physical body helps you feel well and vital. It also helps you bounce back from challenges that you can't plan for, like illness and injuries, including mental and emotional ones.

Mental Health

Your ability to manage your overall mental wellbeing. It includes rational thinking, good decision-making and the ability to manage difficult situations. Often affected by your internal processing, your ability to listen and reason with yourself and others, and then make your choices that work for you.

Emotional Health

Your ability to manage your moods and feelings. Often results from external influences, but also your internal emotional processing. Being able to acknowledge feelings without judgment can help you process them and work through them. How you act and react can be affected by the emotions you feel, but it doesn't have to. The Roman Stoic Epictetus is quoted as having said, "It's not what happens to you, but how you react to it that matters." Your responsibility, your choice.

Confidence

For me, there are two parts to confidence.

Internal confidence, or how you think and feel about yourself, your values, your worth and your self-belief.

External confidence, or how much you believe in your abilities, how comfortable you are with how you look and feel, how sure you are of your abilities and skills.

Both have a huge impact on your BestHealth. The more you explore what affects each of these and the choices you have around improving them for yourself, the more you will feel aligned with your BestLife.

Happiness

A complex, harder-to-pinpoint emotion that involves a range of positive feelings, such as contentment, joy and gratitude. It's often associated with positive life experiences, such as spending time with loved ones, achieving goals or doing things you enjoy.

I like to think that happiness is the baseline of contentment that we have chosen to live our lives by. Other emotions are the peaks and troughs of the excitement and curveballs of life. But we always seek to return to our baseline of happiness. There is an expectation in the world that we are owed happiness and that it is for external influences to provide. If we own and take responsibility for our decisions and actions, then happiness is totally under our control and our choice alone to feel. By having an awareness of how you measure up in these areas, you can quickly and easily see where you could make improvements in your health.

It is great to see that, finally, in 2025, emotional and mental health are at last being acknowledged as key factors in overall health. (Although they do tend to get lumped together). These three are all interlinked, and often what affects one will cause changes in one or both of the others. A really clear example is the brain. Often only associated with mental health, the brain is also a part of our body, and as such, is directly influenced by physical factors such as dehydration and blood flow.

Your Essentials

These seven areas, when combined, make up the majority of physical key components to your BestHealth and also affect aspects of your mental and emotional health. When done consistently and sustainably, the impact is hugely positive.

I will reiterate at this point: I am staying on super high levels, as the focus of this book is your BestLife RoadMap. A full discussion of your BestHealth RoadMap would warrant its own book!

Sleep

A foundational aspect of health. The quality and quantity of sleep we get have a direct link to our physical and mental wellness. Aiming for seven hours a night is optimal, but it will vary by individual. There are many aspects of improving your chances of a great night's sleep. It is vital for the health of your brain, both physically and mentally, as it is the reboot button for your physical computer! I would encourage you to practise a bedtime sleep ritual that has no screens in it and lots of lovely ways to relax. Also, you require a cool, dark room with minimal distractions.

Nutrition

The basics are listed above in the government Eatwell Guide recommendations. However, optimal nutrition would be more detailed and recommendations for individuals will vary widely. What I will state is that what you eat and drink is much more important than when you eat and drink. When you eat and drink is largely a matter of personal preference and will have minimal overall impact on long-term weight loss or gain. Liquids do not have to be entirely water, but be aware of the components of non-water liquids on your health. And no, you don't need special water to stay properly hydrated. Use the colour of your urine to measure your hydration. Aim for a pale yellow daily. The darker it is, the more dehydrated you are.

Foodwise, the Eatwell guidelines above are OK for the first level on our Levels of Life stages. Contrary to lots of trendy diet fads, a combination of all three macronutrients (protein, carbs, fats) in your daily nutrition is beneficial. Experimenting with the balance and timings of your carbohydrates, fats and protein to feel which combination works best for you, your energy and your body can be an interesting learning exercise on how you feel physically and mentally with different combinations.

Daily Movement

Summarised in the government guidelines as "Minimise sedentary time by breaking up periods of inactivity."

Daily movement is key. It relieves the tension in the body that results from maintaining one position for a prolonged period. Physical movement promotes mental movement as the blood flows through the body. It also helps ease stiff joints and is often the solution for general aches and pains. Step counting is only one way to measure how much you move in a day. Many other ways are just as valid: fidgeting, cleaning, shopping, stretching, dancing around the sitting room. The more non-official exercise movement, the better. You and your physical abilities are your only restrictions. Moving little and often is sometimes easier to sustain than a dedicated big push.

Exercise

This is the official version as opposed to the daily movement version. "Be active – at least 150 minutes of moderate intensity per week (increased breathing and able to talk) or at least 75 minutes of vigorous intensity per week (breathing fast and difficulty talking), or a combination of both."

It can be anything that gets your heart rate up. Ideally, something that you actually enjoy. Nothing more soul-destroying than regularly doing something you hate. So whether it's a dance class or dancing around your kitchen, squats whilst the kettle boils or squats in a gym, just be sure to do it.

Flexibility and Mobility

The most neglected of all the physical components! Flexibility is the ability of a muscle to stretch, while mobility is the ability of a joint to move through its full range of motion. For example, flexibility is the ability to touch your toes, while mobility is the ability to squat to a deep depth. Both are important. The easiest way to see where you currently are is to move your body in as many different ways as possible and make a note of anything that feels tight or doesn't go full range. Pay particular attention to anything bordering on or going into pain. Then practise, often. It's really a case of "move it or lose it" when it comes to flexibility and mobility. But never fear, with practice you can often get it back again (to a greater or lesser degree).

Strength

The government's recommendation to build strength at least twice a week barely scratches the surface of why strength is so important and why maintaining your muscle mass is essential. If you could only do one type of exercise, I'd recommend strength training.

Strength training, whether performed with weights, bands, machines or your own body weight, is important for your long-term health. Also known as resistance training, it increases muscular strength, endurance and bone density. It also works on coordination, flexibility and mobility. Depending on the intensity, it works on your cardiovascular health, too. Huge gains for your time and energy investment. Yoga, Pilates, weight training and callisthenics all count. Find one that you enjoy and do that, at least twice a week.

Cardiovascular

Cardiovascular health and training are about how well your heart works when taxed and how fast it recovers. The health of your heart is essential to your BestHealth and your BestLife. Your heart is a muscle and needs its own version of strength training. Regularly making it beat hard and fast, and then recovering quickly, is essential to its continued health. This is the primary reason the exercise guidelines listed above are in place. Doing cardio activities increases your body's blood flow, giving you lots of additional benefits like brain engagement, mood-enhancing hormones, immune system boosting, sleep quality and many more. Find a way that you enjoy and get your 75 to 150 minutes in a week! Making just one change in one of these areas can have a great impact on your BestHealth and BestLife. Imagine the impact of consistently actioning in all seven!

Your Lifestyle

This third Y is all about how the outside world influences you. The more you can rate yourself high in each of these five areas, the more you will rate highly in the Levels of Life. If you can align your core values, which we covered earlier, with these external influences, you will be living a version of your BestLife that works for you.

Family

When considering external influences, family is among the most significant influencers. Not just close family members, but also extended ones and even in-laws. They say that you can't choose your family, but you can choose your friends. It is always worth examining the relationships within your family to see where you feel loved and valued, and where perhaps you do not. Great personal impact can come from putting boundaries in place with those relatives who, even unintentionally, cause you damage and pain.

Friends

Friends are our trusted chosen circle of confidants. They can also be people we get on with in work, a partner's best mate or people we socialise or network with. Friendships have as many layers as family. And can bring as much joy or pain as those family relationships. I am a firm believer that friends are for a reason, a season or a lifetime. Even when a friendship ends, it can be learned from and valued.

I also believe that true friendship is a two-way street. This is often forgotten, and feelings of neglect and hurt can develop when communication is not balanced. The common habit is to continue with a friendship like this long after each party has stopped valuing their part within it, usually because we don't want to hurt their feelings. So we continue at the expense of our own! Choosing your friends and deciding whether to continue your friendships is entirely up to you. Choosing not to continue a friendship is also down to you. Both can help you live your BestLife and practise your BestHealth!

Work

I discussed earlier in the chapter the importance of aligning your brain with your core values and purpose. And work is a huge part of that alignment. Being able to live your values at work means work feels easier and more rewarding. When they are not in alignment, it can feel more challenging. When work means bringing in the money to pay the bills, but you don't enjoy it, it can be a mentally and emotionally challenging experience. When the work environment is not supportive of you, there is more challenge. When you take responsibility for your choices and actions, you can approach a challenge with a more open mind and find a way of seeing and working that can bring some alignment back. For example, working a boring job that gives you a salary and flexible work hours to live your BestLife outside of work is certainly better than working a boring job without the flexibility. Asking what you can do and what you can change can help shift your mindset into a positive-solution thinking approach when work cannot be changed.

Community

Humans have always needed to be part of a community. Historically, this helped us survive the sabre-tooth tigers! Nowadays, the need is still present, but it is fulfilled in various ways. It enables us to feel a part of something and have value. When looking at the community, it will be different for each individual. Many people in my business networking community also have a strong connection through the golf or football community. Neither of which I shall be rushing to participate in. I recently took up kayaking (the slow, leisurely kind!) and am being slowly and leisurely embraced into that community. Being part of any community is an easy way to boost your BestLife.

If you feel disconnected from the community you are in, then detaching could give you the same boost. Examining your place within your community will give you the freedom to choose whether to stay or go.

World

The world is getting smaller and smaller as technology brings us all closer together. The awareness of what is happening in your immediate world, the impact the greater world has on it and the impact you have on the greater world is immense. Messaging comes from all around us about the good, the bad and the ugly in the world. Often, it is hard to discern truth from lies, fact from influence and best interest from greed. It is your responsibility to control where you learn from and how much influence you let affect you. It is also your choice what actions you take for yourself and for the greater good of the world and the planet.

Fact-checking is not glamorous work, but it is vital in the sea of information. Hearing multiple views and choosing your own after fact-checking and consideration is a skill that needs practising. The more you practise, the more confident you will be about what you value in this world and what values of the world you take into your core beliefs.

External influences play a large part in your BestLife. Having an awareness of the impact they play on a daily basis enables you to make choices that help you thrive, whether it be removing something or someone, or even finding them!

Scores on the Doors

Now we have explored the 3Y's of Health. They can be used together with the Levels of Life to build a conscious snapshot of where you are right now. To check in with where you are now on your Best Health, I have created an exercise that will help you listen to your inner voice and gut instinct, tapping into your various levels in a way that works within the cultural environment we are accustomed to in the UK.

This exercise will help you establish where you feel confident and strong, and where you feel weaker and more vulnerable. How you measure yourself comes from within you. From this, you will be able to identify where you want to put more energy to build your BestLife. Using the sliding scale of 1 to 10 for each element (1 being the worst it could be and 10 being as good as you can imagine it getting), you can quickly check in with how you are doing.

Using a quick-fire technique when answering will allow your unconscious mind and gut instinct to drive your answers. There is a time and place for logic, and that is *after* you have completed your scores. The reason behind this is that if you let your logical brain answer, it will start rationalising the answer, but your gut instinct is how you actually feel.

For example, if I measured my daily movement score whilst I'm writing this book, my gut says 3/10, but my rational conscious mind says anywhere from 5 to 7 because I have got up regularly and wandered about. I know that my 3/10 is my true score because on a regular day, when I'm not writing, I move an awful lot more. It is important to have your own measure for this. Do not measure yourself against anyone else around you. Comparison is the thief of joy and also part of the logical brain. And that is not what you want here! Everything you do to move towards living your BestLife has got to be a Win/Win by choice.

All the adult stuff you have to do – things like working to ensure you have enough money to cover your basic needs of shelter and food, the responsibilities of caring for family members – can be a joy and a chore all at the same time!

You can choose *how* you act on those things. There are certain things you can't avoid doing. It is in how you combine those with the things that nurture your soul and build your resilience that enable you to enjoy your life, no matter how many curveballs are thrown at you. This next exercise is super useful for quick check-ins in your life.

Exercise: Scores on The Doors/10

This exercise is designed for you to give yourself your score/10 on your Best Health BestLife. It is a snapshot for learning and awareness. If you don't know where you currently are, you can't make and measure any changes, actions and the impact they have on your BestLife.

Rate yourself on each of the items in the list from 1 to 10 (0 means you're dead). One is the worst it could possibly be (something has to change, and now), while 10 is the best it could be (nothing needs to change currently). Give yourself your scores on the doors. Use your gut instinct. Read the item and write the first number that comes into your head. Do not overthink. If you find yourself having a little internal debate about one, leave it and come back to it.

This exercise, when done well, should take you no more than two minutes to complete. Once you have completed the scores on the doors, look at your scores.

I do this exercise pretty much daily, often in relation to my happiness. If my daily happiness score is a five, I stop and pause. When I'm having the wild moments, I'll go, "Oh, shit, I've done it again," and I'll stop wherever I am, take a breath and ask myself the following: "What's my score? And why is it that number? Which bit have I let go, and what can I do?" Anything below a 6/10 needs my attention and thought.

This is key. When you're scoring on the doors, if your result is below a six, you need to see what you can do to improve it. Don't think if it's a two that you have to choose an action that will take you straight up to a 6/10. The lower the score you are looking at, the more resistance and emotion you may have to raising the score. Instead of going from a 2/10 to a 6/10, think about what could get you to a 3/10 or even a 2.1/10. Any change will help you. The smaller the step you have to take, the more micro the action, the less your reptilian brain is going to fight against it. Remember, all the reptilian brain wants is for you to do the same as you've always done. By making the changes as small as possible, there is less fear involved, and so you are more likely to be able to make the change, enabling you to keep on making more tiny changes.

Scores on The Doors/10

You
- ★ Physical Health
- ★ Mental Health
- ★ Emotional Health
- ★ Confidence
- ★ Happiness

Your Essentials
- ★ Sleep
- ★ Nutrition
- ★ Daily Movement
- ★ Exercise
- ★ Flexibility/Mobility
- ★ Strength
- ★ Cardiovascular

Your Lifestyle
- ★ Family
- ★ Friends
- ★ Work
- ★ Community
- ★ World

How Are You?

Bonus Time

Ask yourself these questions and look for the answers within yourself and within your immediate external environment.

Do you have any obvious areas that you feel need immediate improvement?

What learning can you take away?

What possible actions could you take?

Which areas are you doing well in, and how will you celebrate those numbers?

What emotions have you felt doing this exercise?

Mark on your paper the questions you want to focus on that you'd like to be higher. Put an asterisk or something next to them, reminding you that you want to do some work around it, to reframe or make it work better for you.

Certain things you can't change, but there'll always be a way of changing how you look at it, or an alternative way to boost the score. By carrying out this exercise regularly, you will discover your own balance and be able to see when something is awry and needs attention.

Once you have given yourself a score for each element, you will be able to clearly see where you can take some action to boost yourself. Always think in terms of increasing your score gradually. It is much easier to go from 3 to 4 than it is to go from 3 to 9!

The higher we score, the happier our brain will be.

Look at anything that resonates as low to you and decide if it is currently a high priority.

Do this exercise regularly, especially when you feel out of sorts or out of control.

Part 1: A to Now Wrap Up

The end of this section of the A to Now journey is a great time to consolidate where you have travelled from and what you want to take forward with you on your BestLife.

Digging into your mind to discover the whats, hows, and whys of your current life is a lot to process. It can throw up big questions and possibly leave you feeling a bit (or a lot) overwhelmed.

That is why it is essential we take a moment to review where you are *right now*, taking into consideration all that we have discovered together in Part 1.

- ★ A to Z Map of Your World
- ★ The Brain & Thinking

- ★ Three Levels of Living
- ★ Who are You
- ★ Your Core Values
- ★ Your Purpose
- ★ How Are You?
- ★ The 3Y's to your BestHealth

The awareness you now have of your current way of living is the Road Marker, the flag in the ground, from which we will move forward and build your BestLife RoadMap. Understanding where you are right now and how that is working for you is vital in recognising where you've been and where you want to go.

Before we launch into your next stage, Part Two: Now to Z, let's compile your summary page, detailing where you have come from, what is great, what you want to change and why.

By reviewing with your conscious mind all the information you have pulled from your brain using your inner voice and gut instinct, you will be in the best place to decide what to change so you can make better choices moving

A to Now Wrap-Up

forward. These choices will help keep you on the road to your BestLife.

If you haven't completed the exercises or need to revisit some questions, this is the time to do it. Remind yourself that any self-talk stopping you from completing the exercises is just that pesky reptilian brain wanting to keep you safe.

The more you know why the current picture looks how it does and the reasons for the emotions around it, the more you will be able to build the RoadMap of your BestLife in the coming sections.

The exercises in this section can be repeated regularly so that you never lose your way in this crazy journey of life. By checking in regularly, you can ensure you are always in control of the decisions you make and the actions you take.

Do the work and you will give yourself the best chance to move forward in the direction you want to go, living your best life on your journey to Z. Now is where you place your marker on the road and reset your trip switch for the miles to come.

Exercise: Your Current Road Marker – Summary of A to Now

You are going to look at the work you have done and shuffle some order into it. By creating your Road Marker, you will have a summary of where you are currently at and why, and ideas on where you want your road to take you.

We humans are driven by feelings and emotions first and logic second. I am a strong believer in trusting our gut instincts. It's not led to positive outcomes whenever I haven't in the past.

Knowing that our reptilian brain is trying to override everything else will remind us to check in with all aspects, take a look at the full picture before going with our gut.

If you want to maximise the opportunity for your answers, do this exercise, then sleep on it and revisit the next day. Sleep allows your brain to process the questions fully.

Gather together your answers to the Part One Exercises and then, on a clean piece of paper, create your summary. I suggest putting today's date on it. You may, in the future, want to look back on the road you have travelled to review.

Exercises from Part One - A to Now

- ★ Brain Dump Mind Map
- ★ In and Out of the Box
- ★ What is Important to you
- ★ Your Scores on The Doors

A: Brain Dump Mind Map

Choose one, two or three items you want to look at changing and write them on your RoadMarker summary sheet. Ask yourself these questions about the item you want to change.

Why do you want this change?

How will this change help you thrive?

What impact will this change have on your daily life?

What does this change look like in your daily life?

Handy hint: Write down your instinctual answers and then have a break. Come back to your answers and re-ask yourself the questions. This brings your subconscious and unconscious feelings and emotional mind into play first, and then follows it up with your conscious logical mind rather than the other way around. Write anything. There are no rights or wrongs.

B: In and Out of the Box + What is Important to You?

Write down on your RoadMarker summary sheet your understanding of your current life and values by answering these questions:

What are the three best things about your current life?

What are the three worst things about your current life?

What core values resonate with you?

What is important to you in your life?

C: How Are You?

Looking at the BestHealth section (3 Levels of Living and the 3 Y's), write your answers on the RoadMaker summary sheet for the following questions.

Which were your three highest BestHealth scores and why?

Which were your three lowest scores on the doors and why?

What one, two or three would you like to work on?

A to Now Wrap-Up

D: Scores on the Doors

If you were to give yourself a BestLife overall score on The Door for the life you are living right now, what would it be? (1 being it couldn't get worse and 10 being it couldn't get better). What one thing could you do to move that score a fraction higher?

You have just completed your first Road Marker for your BestLife RoadMap.

You now have:

- ★ a full picture of your life as it currently is
- ★ an awareness of what is working and not working for you
- ★ a current Bestlife Score on the Door
- ★ spied a few roadworks that need detours
- ★ maybe a couple of destinations you no longer want to visit
- ★ an idea of the road you want to travel moving forward

Keep your RoadMarker summary so that you can revisit it in the future and check in on how far you have travelled and whether it is still the right road for you and your BestLife.

Part 2:

Where Could You Go? Now to Z

Where Could You Go? Now to Z

In Part 1, we covered Groundwork: A to Now – where you have come from, your current life and where you are now. We also explored who you are and what you value. We then examined how you currently feel and what you are doing in your life.

Now you get to look forward!

What does your BestLife look like to you? Where could you go? And how will you establish what needs to happen to get there?

So, what does this have to do with your life, your journey and where you are now?

The RoadMarker you are currently on in this Life journey is the box where your reptilian brain feels safe. We discussed this in Part 1, where, in your brain, you were okay but potentially not at your best. You needed to open the lid on this box and bring your current life out into the light, so you could have a good look at it and decide if it is working for you or not.

Opening the lid to the box you are currently living in really helps you to shine a light and see your choices in their true form. Once you know what those choices are, you can open your mind to explore different ways you could be, do and live.

I find it very exciting to help people sort out their shit in their lives. Each day, I help individuals do this from my Shed of Strength or via virtual shed sessions online. I do this as my purpose, and it brings me great joy seeing others live their best life. But I can't help as many as I would like to in this format. This book is my way of sharing that joy to help you do the same.

This next step is my favourite part: It is full of excitement and exploration because it is where you get to imagine and create the RoadMap to your own BestLife.

Where Are You on the RoadMap of Life?

We will first set some groundwork before we get stuck in. It is important for us both to be on the same page when it comes to the creation of your RoadMap. I am going to share with you my different way of looking at life and how you can plan for your future.

Normally, when you look at where your life is right now, it is often in terms of your age and where you are in your community, your society and your culture. That's how you have probably been trained to measure your success in life: by comparing yourself with other people. How old you are and how well you've been doing for your age. How much stuff have you got? How much money are you earning? What level are you at in your job?

And I dislike comparison with others as a measure of how successful we are in our lives, so I've changed it, reframed it to sit better within my values and ethos of the RoadMap to your BestLife. There are two certainties in life: You are born and you die, and neither of those things you can avoid. You certainly don't get a choice in the first, and you rarely get a choice in the last. But the bit in the middle, you do have a lot of control over. You choose your actions and the path you take, and where you go and who you go there with.

I want you to imagine your life as a map of the UK.

In my head, I am imagining one of those old, A3-sized map books that used to kick about in the car when we were kids! It had a huge title on the front: *A–Z Map of Great Britain*.

Now, picture a point on that map and label it A. This is your starting point, the day you were born.

Then pick a point on that map as far away as you can find and label it Z. This is the day you die. A certainty in events but not in time.

Now look between those two points. There is a whole load of miles and a multitude of routes you can take to get from

Where Are You on the Roadmap of Life?

A to Z. Those are all the other letters of the alphabet – 24 letters to be precise; 24 letters that you get to decide what they mean to you, where they have taken you up to now and where they are going to take you in the future.

This is where I ask you to think about where you are on your A to Z of life.

Those 24 letters that you've got to play with can be measured in any way, shape or form, where you are.

These are measures you could use to determine your position on the 24-letter Life alphabet:

You could do it on your own terms, and not necessarily via the conventional routes of life.

You could consider what you have achieved on your bucket list and what you still want to do.

You could look at how much you've lived your life by other people's agendas versus your own agenda.

If I were to determine where I am now using age as a measure, I would probably put myself at S, two-thirds of the way through. I find this quite miserable because it doesn't leave me with many letters to write (also, it makes me feel old and grown up!). So I changed my scale and measured my "location" to where I was against "things I want to do." And that landed me right before an M, which aligns better with how I view my life. I've done quite a lot that I'm really properly chuffed with. There's still so much I want to achieve and do, both professionally and personally. So I reckon I'm about halfway through.

So what's your letter? Where are you on your A to Z?

Exercise: Your Position Now On Your A-to-Z Map of Life

This exercise, although an objective look at your life, can feel a bit brutal. The purpose is to shine a light on where you are and how you are living, and put it into the context of where you have been and where you are going.

A is your Start Point.

Z is your End Point.

B to Y is your Life Journey.

A BCDEFGHIJKLMNOPQRSTUVWXY**Z**

Choose the scale that you will measure your life against. This could be age, bucket list, life purpose or experiences.

Where would you say you are now?

Pick a letter of the alphabet that represents where you currently are in your A to Z of life.

As you already have starting and ending letters, you have 24 other letters in the English alphabet to play with. How you play with these letters is up to you. Remember, this is *your* system, *your* plan for *your* life. I am here to show you the BestLife framework. It is up to you to take the framework and adapt it to work in the best way possible for you.

I deliberately don't use numbers for this exercise, as the tendency is to think about how long you will live. Nobody really knows the answer to that. Plus, it triggers that pesky reptilian brain into action. Don't overthink it, just give yourself a letter and know what your scale of measurement is so you can revisit it later.

Write it down before you forget!

Where Are You on the Roadmap of Life?

The Good, the Bad and the Ugly

Looking at your Now point, we are going to look at where you currently are with regards to the good, the bad and the ugly! It's important to look at what's going great, what's not so great and what you literally want to never ever do or be a part of ever again. This part is about getting all the shit out of your head and dumping it on to your table, having a good rummage around, deciding what's essential to you and your BestLife and how it's going to go back into your head.

We started this process in Part 1 with the Brain Dump exercise around what you currently do each day in your life. The next stage is to reflect on all the large and small things you have already experienced in your life and choose whether you would like to experience them again (Good), never experience them again (Bad) or experience them in a different but improved way (Ugly).

I will give you an example of each from my life.

The Good

As a kid, I lived up in Derbyshire close to the River Trent. My uncle was a kayak instructor, so my brother and I had access to boats to play in. We would often carry these boats on a weekend and go play on the river, without adults! My uncle made sure we were trained and safe to do so. These were before inflatable boats were a thing, and those fibreglass boats were heavy, cumbersome and a lot of work to get to the water.

But I don't really remember the hard work. I just remember the freedom to float, paddle and race. The feeling of being in charge of myself without anyone else telling me what to do. Seeing beautiful countryside in a way that most don't see it. So when I was looking at my Good experiences for this exercise, this came up as a powerful one, even though I hadn't really river-kayaked since then!

The Bad

When I first met my now-husband (way back in 1992), he spent his weekends either on Salisbury Plain as a member of the Territorial Army or down in and around Plymouth as a crew member on a racing boat. Between these two, I didn't get to see him much. I then decided to take up one of his hobbies! I didn't fancy getting cold and wet on Salisbury Plain, so I chose sailing instead. This led me down a path of experiences over many years that I will never forget. I had to learn to sail separately because the crew didn't take beginners. Then I managed to get on the boat to help bring it back from cross-channel races, and finally, I made the cut as a spare. That meant I could race when the regular crew was down a member.

When I tell this story, people often think it sounds amazing. And yes, I had some unforgettably amazing moments sailing. I also met and remain friends with many of the people I sailed with. But it was a feat of endurance for me. You see, I get really travel-sick. And on the sea, it is at its worst! For the first 12 hours of *every* trip, I was sick. No amount of medicine or pressure point bands would help. The only thing that cured it was time! It got to the point where everyone just accepted that I would sleep up on deck wrapped around the winch, only moving when I had to do some winching! Recently, it was suggested that we do another sailing trip together with some of our old sailing buddies. I thought long and hard about it…and said no! Although the times we had were mostly amazing, I do not need to spend my precious time being sick! There are other adventures I can have. On a river, in a kayak!

The Ugly

One of the mainstays of my life has been walking, uphill and down dale. I have climbed the three highest mountains in the UK, done the Yorkshire Three Peaks five or so times, climbed

Mt. Toubkal and managed to get back down from a full panic attack after falling at the top!

Walking has been a part of my health journey, bringing me back to life after my black years. I am known for taking head reset walks, angry walks, walks to simply be out in nature and walks with the spaniel pack that we have. Unfortunately, I have had to deal with several physical health cards since 2020, which has meant I am now unable to walk very far at all. The joy and therapy of walking is not currently part of my life. Frustrating though this is, I still need all the experiences these past walks have given me. So my Ugly is not being able to walk far at all, but knowing I will find a way to get it back into my life in some way, shape or form.

To choose where you want your BestLife to lead you means you have to look at what has gone by and see if you want to do it again, never do it again or do a modified version. It is also important that you know your reasons why. Life is too short for regrets. One way to not have regrets is to choose what you do or don't do, and know exactly why that is a great choice for you.

So let's get stuck in and have a look at *your* Good, Bad and Ugly moments.

Exercise: The Good, the Bad, the Ugly

On a fresh piece of paper, write your 3 headings:

GOOD   BAD   UGLY

You are going to note down all the good, bad and ugly things that have happened so far in your life that you can remember underneath each of those headings. Don't think too hard about details. This is emotion-driven driven so instant thoughts pop up from the depths of your mind. Go with your gut. What has happened in the past from A (the day you were born) to Now? Consider anything that's affected your life in a good way, a bad way or an ugly way. Remember, this is your Roadmap, so it needs to work for you. If the words "good," "bad" and "ugly" don't resonate with you, choose different words that do. For example, "love," "hate" and "could be better."

Also, it is worth noting at this point that what you feel is good can also feel bad at different times. You can absolutely put the same thing on two lists, because it can be a great thing and a not-so-great thing combined. There are no rules. For example, you could really enjoy the quality time you get with an elderly relative, but equally find the commitment to always be there for them challenging. This process should help you document everything that is currently affecting you, allowing you to review and decide what is best serving you.

If you get stuck, use your Brain Dump Exercise results from Part One. Another great way is to start from your earliest memory and move through your life, recalling all the experiences you have had and putting them under a heading.

What is Your Agenda?

In the context of this book and your ability to live your BestLife, Your Agenda is something that you set, through your own choice or somebody else's, that steers your choices and actions throughout your day and ultimately your life.

There's a quote that really resonates with me, and if you use this, it will help you realise where your boundaries are. The quote is this:

If you don't have your own Agenda, you will be living your life by somebody else's Agenda.

Every time you go, "I'm sick and tired of doing this." Ask yourself, whose agenda is that? Is that your agenda? Are you choosing that? Or are you doing it because somebody else has chosen you to do it? And do you want to do it?

On the Good, Bad and Ugly exercise you completed at the beginning of Part 2, those situations are often the ugly ones.

How to Find and Create Your Agenda

Two exercises are particularly important in contributing valuable information to help you create your own Agenda. They were covered in Part 1.

The first is the "What is important to you" exercise, which explores the core beliefs you need to align with to make your BestLife easier and flow better. The second is the Brain Dump exercise: What you do in a day. This is all your adulting stuff. When you're looking at your Agenda in terms of how you value yourself and how other people value you, this daily stuff is often forgotten.

There is a lot of talk about the mental load of life. But how does this show up in your life? For most people, a process occurs internally, often represented by an internal dialogue. This dialogue happens daily throughout your life.

For example: Shall I? Shan't I? Should I? I shouldn't do that. I feel guilty about that. Who will do it if I don't? I must do it because nobody else will. What's for dinner?

When do I need to do it? Who's home or away? Who likes what? And so on.

All the things that happen in a day – the processes, the decisions, the actions, the reactions – they all go through an internal dialogue and influence our Agenda. There is also a lot of external influence on your daily activities and to-do lists, but your internal dialogue is where you ultimately choose the actions you take.

The Two Voices

I like to think we have two internal voices that contribute to this internal dialogue.

Voice 1: The Loud Shouty Voice

The loud, shouty voice tells us what we should and shouldn't do: "Don't do that," "That's what kids do." Or, "you shouldn't feel like that because it's your fault." It's the "stop being so lazy and get on with it" voice. It's that big, loud, horrible and shouty voice that censors your thoughts and actions and stops you from listening to your gut and doing the actions you actually want to do. This is the voice that often dominates.

It is also the voice that is mainly influenced by external factors in life. It's often the voice we hear the most, as it is *so loud*. A bit like the teenager who wants something that you really struggle to reason with!

It is important to note here that the Loud Shouty Voice isn't evil or wrong. It is just a manifestation of your internal and external influences and expectations. It is closely aligned with the reptilian brain and wants you to stay safe by doing all the stuff that has kept you intact in the past. Like you would a teenager, acknowledging that you hear the Loud Shouty Voice will help quieten it down. After all, we all want to be listened to. But that doesn't mean you have to do what the Loud Shouty Voice tells you to do!

Voice 2: The Quiet Inner Voice

And then there's another voice inside us. Some call it gut instinct. I call it our Quiet Inner Voice. Our true internal voice of what we really believe and think, value and want. This voice is a lot quieter. It often gets drowned out by the Loud Shouty Voice. But it is worth listening to because it is your voice of truth. And if you train yourself to hear it and pay attention to it, you will be so much more in alignment with your true core values. This Quiet Inner Voice has been shouted over for years by its noisy, blustering and judgmental counterpart, the Loud Shouty Voice, so much so that often it can't be heard without concentrated effort to tune in to it.

When you train yourself to tell the loud, shouty voice to shut up for a bit, you will start to hear your very own quiet but confident voice speak with your deep core values and beliefs. Doing so allows you to make decisions that work for you and with you. When you start asking your Quiet Inner Voice questions and take action on its confident answers, you will be amazed at how much easier your decisions and actions become. Your life choices and daily decisions will become much more aligned to what you value, leading to greater happiness in your life and a much less bumpy road on which you live your BestLife.

When you learn to listen to your Quiet Voice, it can be scary. Those first few times you take action on that second voice can be challenging. As with doing anything new, your reptilian brain can have a wobble on the safety front and throw up obstacles on why you shouldn't take action. But by listening to this quietly confident inner voice, you can build a positive value-based case to reassure your pesky reptile that this is for the benefit of your own safety and that not following this road will lead to more unhappiness and danger.

I lived a prime example of exactly this.

In 2019, I had an episode where I was really, really poorly. It was the weirdest thing I've ever experienced in the whole of my life, and I've experienced quite a lot!

We had spent two weeks in Italy camping with the kids when they were teenagers, and this episode happened as we were driving back in the Land Rover Defender that we use for our travelling. It's not the most enjoyable vehicle for long mileage on tarmac roads, but we love it and are accustomed to the non-luxury conditions.

Halfway back to the UK, in France, I started to get a headache. By the time we stopped for the night, I was struggling to see. Before this, I had had migraines, but this was different. It was just unbelievable pain.

I tried to go for dinner with the family, but had to leave before the end as my brain felt like it was in a vice. And no amount of painkillers or migraine medicines could touch it.

The next morning, we were back in the car. I started to feel weirdly out of my body. And then my body just shut down. I remember travelling with my head in my son's lap with a coat over my head all the way home. Movement hurt, light hurt, all external stimuli hurt. My body shut down, but my mind did not.

What is Your Agenda?

We got home and I lay on top of my bed for the next five days and nights, unable to do anything. Every sound, smell, touch, taste and light hurt. I had an eye shield to block out all the light, but the weight of it hurt. I had to lie on top of the bed because anything over me felt super heavy and claustrophobic. For a week, I didn't eat, I couldn't read, listen or do anything.

Even though my body had stopped because it couldn't cope with the pain, my mind was still alert and working. Because my mind was alert, I was hyper-focused on the situation happening to me. My Loud Shouty Voice was panicked. My reptilian brain was freaking out with the complete unknown of the condition happening to me.

I had to turn my attention and mind away from what was happening. I had to look internally for another way to survive this. I had to find a way through the pain, a way to cope and survive until either the pain stopped or we could find a solution.

I had to dig deep for some kind of survival method. It was so dark and I struggled to find my way. And that is when I discovered the miracle of my internal Quiet Voice. I had to go really deep inside myself to find a place where I was going to survive what I was experiencing.

I spent hours each day and night talking to this quiet voice that I had buried inside of me. Holding conversations on life, the universe and everything, taking past experiences apart and learning from them and creating better stories to tell myself.

It was the weirdest experience of my life, very painful and uncomfortable. But it was the most liberating and empowering experience, too. Knowing that I had the power, my power, to get through and out the other side of this bizarre and challenging physical experience, all I had to do was listen and act on what my inner quiet voice knew to be the right thing for me.

Externally, nobody in my family knew what to do. Nobody could help me. I was in this internal hellstorm, and the only anchor I had was me. The only way to survive was by distracting myself from the pain and drilling down into that inner resource and learning about myself.

By the fifth day, I was able to move enough for my husband to drive me to the A&E. By this time, I had started to recover.

I still to this day don't know what the cause of the physical pain was. However, I do know that the experience taught me that I possess immense resilience within me and a

What is Your Agenda?

strong belief in what I'm capable of. I know that my inner quiet voice is always with me. Whenever I am confronted with challenges, both internally and externally, I know I possess the inner resilience to not only survive but also to thrive.

Now, when I am challenged or have a decision to make, I always take a moment to ask myself what I need to do. I listen carefully to the answers I receive from this incredible, quiet voice that is me and the essence of who I am. When I choose to act on those answers, it is pretty much always the right and easy option for me.

I tell this story because we all absolutely have this amazing inner quiet voice inside of us that has our best interests at heart. It can change our lives if we simply tune in and listen to it.

Finding and listening to your own quiet voice, your gut instinct, takes practice and time. The more you practise, the better you get at hearing and listening. The better you get at listening to your own quiet voice, the more you will choose actions that align with it. The more choices you make that align with your quiet inner voice, the more you will feel like life is working for you. And the more you practise all of that, the smoother your BestLife Road will be.

Living your life by checking in with your inner quiet voice is hugely empowering. When you tune in and listen to it, you realise this important lesson: You get to choose what actions you take and how you act. It is up to you to take that responsibility. If you choose to live your life by other people's agenda, doing all the things that are expected of you and none that you choose for yourself, it can lead to burnout and the emotional, mental and physical implications of complete overwhelm.

I truly believe that because I hadn't listened to (or ignored) my inner quiet voice and spent years living my life for others, not taking personal responsibility for my own needs and wants, I reached a brick wall that stopped me in my tracks. My physical body shut down and forced me to deal with the mental and emotional disconnect.

What happens when you break?

What happened to all my commitments when I couldn't move for five days? They didn't get done.

Did anybody die? Nobody died.

Did I still have a business? Yes, I still had a business.

What is Your Agenda?

So when you are putting your value on yourself, you have to bear in mind what happens if you're not looking after yourself? Is that important?

Because you've got to be sure that all the decisions you make, and every responsibility you take for your happiness, are things you are actively choosing.

If you're not choosing them, somebody else is choosing them for you.

Every time you agree to respond to a text straight away, that is giving somebody else your power.

Every time you don't ask somebody else to cook the meal for you when they've been doing other stuff and you've been working, that is your choice.

You have to take responsibility for your choices. This is where you go, the things that you need to do, the non-negotiables, looking after children, looking after elderly people. How does that look? Does it work for you or are you just doing what they want you to do?

Exercise: Create and Keep Your Agenda

Give yourself the gift of a quiet space with no distractions and 15 minutes of your undivided attention.

You are going to start listening for and to your Quiet Inner Voice. It is often heard behind the emotions of the Loud Shouty Voice. Having no distractions will help you listen carefully.

Collect in front of you the following exercises you have already completed

- ★ Your Road Marker Summary
- ★ Brain Dump Mind Map
- ★ What Is Important to You
- ★ Scores on the Doors
- ★ The Good, the Bad, the Ugly

One exercise at a time, slowly read through the answers you have given. Pay attention to any emotion that you feel as you read through. When you feel something, it is your sign to pause and acknowledge that emotion, and to ask yourself why it is there. When you do this, you can start to hear the real truth behind an answer.

Here is an example.

On my Brain Dump Mind Map, I had written this task: finding the missing items my family can't find. When I looked at it, it created a frustrated anger inside of me. I was always stopping what I was doing to go find the lost thing. I asked the question: Why can't they just find their own stuff? My answer, from my Quiet Inner Voice, was "Because you have always found it for them. They haven't learned the finding skill because they have never had to." My truth? I had voluntarily taken on the "find it" task rather than allowing them to learn the responsibility themselves. My Agenda, in response to this task, is now to allow them to properly search whilst I continue on with my tasks. Amazingly, once I started sticking to my Agenda, they started learning the "find it" skill, and they can now all find the missing items too! So now I can write on my Agenda: "My time on my tasks is as important as theirs, so I will continue doing what I was doing."

My Agenda Summary

As you work through each exercise, jot down on a sheet of paper, under the heading My Agenda Summary, anything that you learn about yourself, and how and why those feelings are there, and any decision you make on:

- ★ Boundaries you need to uphold
- ★ Priorities of your life and your to-do tasks
- ★ Values that you won't compromise
- ★ Where will you compromise, and where will you not

When you are happy with what you have written, share it with those in your life who it affects. It will help them understand why you no longer work to their agenda at the price of yours! Clear communication of our Agenda, Boundaries and Values means less push back when you say "No!" and more enthusiasm when you say "Yes!"

Look to the Future

Now that we have looked at where you have come from and you have your summary for your journey so far from A to Now, it is time to look forward to the future and what that looks like for you.

You cannot have a BestLife if you haven't looked forward as well as backwards. It is important to know where you want to go, what you want to experience and what you want to achieve. Without that, you will be wandering aimlessly without a route map to follow. How will you know whether you are even moving forward? Without a destination in mind to move you from one place to another, you may end up going around in circles, or worse, taking a path you didn't want to take because you were just following the traffic!

This section, Now to Z, will look at where you want to go and how much of the past journey (your A to Now) you want to take into the future with you.

This is your chance to choose your next actions so that your focus is on the BestLife for *you*.

The Impact of You and Your Personal Choice

How important are you?

Do you think it matters whether you are happy in your life?

What impact does thriving have on your life?

The impact you have on everyone around you cannot be underestimated. Only you can choose your actions, and the ripples of those actions affect all those around you in a greater or lesser way. How that affects them will change and create their own ripples. It is known as the butterfly effect: A chaos theory concept coined by meteorologist Edward Lorenz in the 1960s that describes how small changes can lead to big consequences.

Look to the Future

Not only do your actions affect others and create those ripples, but your choices of actions create those ripples within you and your BestLife, too.

Often, life is lived at full speed, and you don't get the opportunity to stop and assess whether the full speed is taking you where you want to go. In this section of the book, you will have the opportunity to take your foot off the accelerator, park up for a bit and take a break from the journey and give yourself time to breathe and dream about how the journey ahead could look.

Many of us have been brought up to put others first, and that it is selfish to spend time on ourselves, for ourselves. There have been mottos of "Keep On Carrying On," "Put Up & Shut Up" and "Don't Complain" as there are people worse off than you.

This mindset has led to whole generations getting through life with no expectation of actually being happy or having fun. I swear this is why the UK has such a drinking culture: to allow individuals to blow off steam or hide from the shit that life can be.

Go back to the Everything You Do Mind Dump exercise with your smiley face in the middle and all your responsibilities around the outside. You are central to all those responsibilities. And if you are thriving, then you are able to take all of those commitments in your stride.

If you are not thriving, however, you will struggle to complete some of your responsibilities, whilst the ones you are doing will have less satisfaction upon completion. You are more likely to get stressed or ill, or drop off the great habits that help you thrive. Chances are, you could start down a slippery slope, coping and then not coping with all the demands on you!

You are super important to all those responsibilities. Who will do it if you cannot?

The priority is to ensure that you are in the best place for you, so that you can give your best to all the tasks and demands on your time and energy.

And you can feel happy while you do them!

Let me share another part of my story with you.

Between 2001 and 2009, in my 30s with two young kids, I was doing all the things. I prioritised my kids' health and wellbeing, and ensured they had everything they needed to grow into smart, healthy, well-balanced and independent individuals. They were my main focus.

Because of my depression and anxiety, I didn't leave the house unless it was for the children – play dates, school, etc. When I left the house, I put my best face on and pushed myself out there so that my kids didn't miss out. I avoided going out during the day unless I absolutely had to. It took so much of my energy to pull my act together and get through these activities that when I got back home, I was exhausted. But I would still have the home responsibilities to complete. Everything was super hard work.

But I was still doing all the responsibilities.

I daren't drop a ball because that would mean I have completely failed.

I was exhausted all the time, and because I feel guilty about any time I take away from the children, I didn't do anything for myself. The most was grabbing 30 minutes to read a fiction book to take me to a different place for a while – and that would be late at night when everyone was asleep! Every once in a while, I would escape: Go out, drink too much, dance the night away, come home late and spend the next day on the sofa recovering and being completely incapable of doing all the things. The night would allow me to blow off steam, but then the next day, I would beat myself up for not being able to function.

Clearly not a thriving life!

In 2009, I looked at a picture of myself taken on my husband's 40th birthday. I didn't recognise myself. In the picture, and from the outside, I look happy. I'm laughing and, on the face of it, having the best time. But that wasn't how I was feeling on the inside: I was lost, hunting for my identity, struggling to remember who Sara was before she had kids. I was in a really bad and unhappy place.

It took looking at this picture for me to realise something had to change, and it had to come from within me. I was at a fork in the road, with one direction leading to more sadness and the other potentially leading the way to a better life for me. I had to start discovering who I was and what I truly wanted in life. I recognised that this couldn't be all there was in life. That there must be some real fun and happiness out there for me.

It was at this point that I looked for somebody to help me.

I remember Googling for hours, looking for just the right thing. I didn't know what or who I was looking for, but I would know when I found it.

I *didn't* find it!

Look to the Future

So I decided to find my own way back to me and my best life, by myself. Slowly, through many false turns and dead ends, I found my way through my maze of unhappiness and found my path back.

I did this by taking responsibility for my own choices and actions and regularly checking in on my life. The Scores on the Doors exercise from the previous section came from this experience.

Are these actions currently working for me? What did I need to tweak or change? If I continue down this path, where am I likely to end up? What resources do I need to keep on track?

It took from 2009 to 2016 for me to get myself back to where I felt like myself, where I felt like I was thriving. The sadness, hopelessness and invisibility I had previously felt were being replaced by positivity and a hopeful outlook on the future.

It was truly marvellous!

And the beauty of this journey was that I was now fulfilling my responsibilities and tasks with purpose and often with a smile. I was able to go outside just because I wanted to, which I did often.

I had a clear idea of what my BestLife could look like and a plan for how to get there and keep thriving as I continued down the road.

It was a completely different way of living my life.

And it had been chosen and created *by* me, *for* me.

I was responsible for my thriving life!

And the impact of my thriving was visible throughout my family. It wasn't until I was going outside regularly that I realised my kids' behaviour also changed. They went from kids who hung out in their rooms and didn't often ask to go out, to kids who were out and about making friends, enjoying hobbies and clubs.

I hadn't realised the impact of my functioning depressive lifestyle had had on these two beautiful kids.

But as I thrived, so did they!

They fed off the energy I was giving out.

Humans are creatures of energy, and energy feeds energy. So, who you surround yourself with will have a direct effect on you and your energy. My energy through my

Look to the Future

depression had led to my kids' energy being toned down and closed off.

As soon as I allowed myself to live again in my best way, it reflected back on my kids' behaviour and joy in life.

Why do I tell you all this?

Because *you* are important. And it's important for you to realise the impact that fact has not just on your life, but on everyone you come into contact with.

Imagine you are walking into a crowded room. Perhaps you're networking for business, attending a party or a family gathering. Stand in the doorway and look into the room.

There will be a person there who appears to be enjoying themselves, having a good time with interesting conversations. Maybe they look friendly and approachable. They definitely look comfortable in their own skin. They sure look happy.

There will also be the person looking like they want to be anywhere but in that room. Perhaps they look grumpy; perhaps their body language suggests they are disagreeing or arguing. They don't look approachable, and you certainly don't want to get stuck making polite conversation with them.

Which of these individuals are you drawn to? Who are you going to walk over to and spend time with?

And who will you avoid like the plague?!

Chances are, the one you are drawn to is living a version of their best life. The one you're avoiding probably isn't living their best life, not even close!

How draining is it when you have a conversation with a negative person? And how uplifting can it feel to have a conversation with a positive person?

Which person do you want to be?

Now, I am not saying you have to be positive and upbeat all the time. That is not human nature. We feel all the feelings. There is a fine line between love and hate. Between laughing and crying. Part of thriving means embracing all the feelings, not hiding from them and squishing them down into their own box, pretending they don't exist. But how we then choose to act on those feelings has a direct impact on our happiness and the happiness of all those around us.

It is Not Selfish to Be Selfish

Doing what makes you happy is not a selfish act.

It is the ultimate selfless act.

We cannot help or give to others if we haven't first helped and given to ourselves, allowing ourselves to thrive.

The common scenario is that most people don't choose how they live their lives. When you go through life on autopilot, moving from one year to the next and falling into one job or another, you pass the responsibility for your life and your happiness to others. There is no plan or choice around your life. This can make you feel dissatisfied and unmotivated at best, and severely depressed, anxious and miserable at worst.

If you carry on living like this, life may be OK, but will it be the best life it could be? You would be back to living in that box with no idea of the potential for your best life. Your reptilian brain would be happy because you are doing nothing to trigger fear, but the slippery slope into unhappiness and depression may go undetected until a crisis hits.

How, from this state of being, can you give your best self to others?

You are important, too important to leave the potential for your happiest life at the door of someone else. You are too important to yourself and to everyone you choose to be around. Your life is too precious to leave all the letters between A and Z as someone else's choice.

So, how can you make sure it is *your* life you are living?

The exercises from Part 1: A to Now will help you keep a watchful eye on your scores on the doors and the actions you are taking that are either leading you in the right direction or pulling you off course.

My advice to you is to regularly carry out the Current RoadMarker Exercise from Part 1. By doing this, you can then actively choose what elements of your life you want to keep, what elements you need to keep and what elements you want to get rid of. This will help you stay on track and also notice when you are deviating or getting a bit lost.

Without this check-in, you do not have the knowledge and control over what happens in your life. You won't find out who or what has been stealing your best life!

How Do You See Yourself?

This is a game-changer of a chapter!

In this part of the book, we need to look at how you see yourself. By this, I mean the perceptions you have of who you are, what type of person you are and what you think is right or wrong. Essentially, we need to look at the internal dialogue that runs as a constant filter on your day-to-day life. As you have seen from the Part 1 exercise on your Core Values and from Part 2: Your Agenda and The Two Voices, it is really important that you take a good look inside yourself. This helps you identify your unique opinions, strengths and weaknesses. How you talk to yourself when you're happy, sad, challenged or excited is an important component of living your best life.

When you looked at your core values, you may have seen the influence others have on you. Your internal values and these external influences help shape your perspective on life. They are the filters through which we see life and what can affect our decision-making. The expression "living life through rose coloured glasses" can be used as a picture of seeing life as all positive, even when it is not.

Think of these filters as the glasses you wear to see the road you are travelling on. A pair of polarised sunglasses helps with clarity of vision against the glare of the sun, but will hinder your ability to see some screens within your car. Your life is experienced through the filters that you have learned, which are shaped by your life experiences, choices and values. These filters shape your perspective of the world around you, and from them you create the life you live. Some will help you, and some will hinder you. And some will do both. Without an awareness of what glasses you are wearing, you can't take your glasses on and off when required to help you see the best direction.

Our filters start loading into our brains from a very early age and are formed by our internal and external experiences of life. Not all of them are sensible or serve us well. Some are rational, such as a fear of heights (or drops), which serves as a filter designed to keep us safe.

How Do You See Yourself?

And some are learned irrational filters. For example, I have a filter that moths are terrifying. There is no evidence that moths are actually dangerous. But I learned from a very early age from my grandmother and mother's reactions and behaviours around moths that there was something to fear in them. To this day, I choose not to spend time anywhere near them!

How do those filters work? Everything you see, hear or feel gets put through the filters of past learnings and, in turn, becomes a logged experience and thought in your brain. Filters are useful because they help you navigate life by providing options in each situation. They help you quickly decide between safe and not safe, good and bad, fun and horrible!

However, we're often unaware of how our filters shape our perspective and how we live our lives and work around others.

If you were walking through a door and another person was coming through after you, you might choose to hold the door open for them. One of your filters in this case could be politeness and manners, such as holding a door open for another. If manners are an important filter for you, this action would be second nature, and you wouldn't think twice about it. If that individual then didn't say thank you after you held the door open, then your perspective would be that this individual was terribly rude. The judgment would be made without conscious thought and without any actual knowledge of that person!

Our filters affect our perspective on the world throughout each and every action. They can lead us to make snap judgments, based on our filters, which may not be the same as another person's.

So, you see, your filters can both limit you and guide you. Filters can lead to prejudices that cause you to ignore things that oppose them, and to bond with people who share the same. Someone who dislikes a person might be dismissive of their ideas. And someone who truly loves a person may adopt their beliefs and perspectives.

Being aware of your own can help you understand yourself better, view how others see things differently and free you to make conscious choices with your actions. Being aware of your filters can help you learn about what you find important and make decisions in support of those beliefs. Being aware will also help you have more constructive conversations and meaningful relationships, which ultimately lead to a healthier and happier life.

How Do You See Yourself?

To unearth your filters, it is key to listen carefully to your Loud Shouty Voice. You know the voice. It can often be found saying negative things like:

> "Well, they got that wrong / don't know what they are on about / have no idea!"

> "You can't wear that because it's not appropriate / too bright / too tight!"

> "I can't do that because I'm too old / weak / fat / broken."

Filters applied by our Loud Shouty Voice tend to shout very loudly in a negative way.

Filters can also be triggered by other people, often by those you like or respect, who tell you you shouldn't, you can't or you mustn't.

I spent the vast majority of my life unconsciously living with these filters:

> "Don't show off!"

> "Don't be too much!"

> "Be seen, not heard."

> "Don't state your opinion unless you can back it up with evidence."

It meant that, at that stage in my life, I never managed to live fully as my authentic self. I often felt pretty crappy about myself, and I certainly wasn't thriving.

For example, in my early 20s, sometime around 1989, I was told by a boss that I was too aggressive in my opinions. This one statement, combined with my formative years growing up in a noisy, opinionated house, meant I put a filter on to not share my opinions with others. There was much less conflict if I always appeared neutral in any potential conflict situation. This led to me not standing up for myself when I found myself in an emotionally abusive relationship. I was so good at masking and hiding my true feelings that nobody knew. And even after I managed to leave that relationship, it was years before I could acknowledge out loud what I had been through.

But once I found these filters, recognised them as such and that they were not serving me, I was able to choose to remove or change them to filters that *did* serve me.

Now I am much happier living with these substitute filters:

> "I am enough."

How Do You See Yourself?

"Being me is awesome."

"Being the centre of attention is fun."

"My voice and opinion are my own and belong to nobody else."

The easiest way to find those limiting filters is to pay attention to anything that creates conflict within you. Try to reflect on whether you are holding an assumption, conclusion or opinion as your truth. Is your belief actually true? Or are you making a presumption? If you struggle to identify these filters on your own, try sharing your filter stories with others and listening for and acknowledging how they may see things differently.

This is clearly demonstrated by one of my superstar clients. I shall call her Ruby. Ruby came to my half-day SOS Life Workshop in 2018. We hadn't met before she attended, but Ruby was at the point in her life where she needed to do something differently and had decided to take action.

Ruby's filters were telling her that she needed to lose weight and get fit to be happy in her life. Ruby ran her own business, was coming out of a long-term relationship and finding her feet in her new independent life. Ruby's brain was busy providing all the evidence through her filters of why doing the same as she had always done was safer than doing anything different.

Ruby made the statement that she wanted to explore swimming clubs, but her perception was that she couldn't – because she was the wrong shape, wasn't fit enough and people would judge her. Her filters were limiting her ability to move towards something she wanted to try. Once she recognised these thoughts as the limiting filters that they were, she was able to remove the filter that told her she was "wrong" for swimming and that people would judge her. By doing this, Ruby freed herself to give swimming a go. Six months after the workshop, I caught up with Ruby, who was living her best life, taking part in triathlons. Ruby said to me, "The people in the club weren't scary or judgmental but supportive, enabling and kind." Now, in 2025, Ruby is still eliminating limiting filters, exploring her potential and has added Olympic lifting and strength training to her arsenal of awesomeness!

Needless to say, Ruby has decided that what she weighs has no bearing on what makes her happy in her life!

How Do You See Yourself?

Exercise: Find Your Filters

It's time to look at how your filters affect how you live and the choices you make. This exercise will help you clarify where some of your potential filters lie and how they affect your thinking. It will also open your mind to potential alternative ways of thinking and new ideas around what actions you could choose to take, once you are aware of them.

Internal and External Filters

Draw two columns on a piece of paper. In the first column, make a list:

All the things you can't do

All the things you won't do

All the things you could do

All the things you want to do

In the second column, write down:

Why you can't

Why you won't

Why you could

Why you want to

How you could

Pay attention as you write to the internal voices that will either shout or whisper at you as you write. Those are the filters through which you are answering the questions. Underneath your columns, write down what filters have come up for you. Then you can decide to keep the helpful filters and either change or discard the limiting ones!

As you can see, knowing your filters alongside understanding your Core Values (from Part 1: A to Now) really highlight how you view the world through your own eyes. They allow you to see the influences, both internal and external, that shape your views. Without this awareness, you can continue living life and be completely unaware that you are living, not for yourself and your own beliefs, but through the values and beliefs of others.

How liberating it is to know that you and only you are in control of what you choose to believe and the filters through which you view life. Once you learn and practise this, you will always be able to have your own filter through which to accept or reject others' opinions and agendas. And so you will lead a life of your choice, your BestLife!

Your bestLife: Past, Present and Future

In this chapter, you will move through the various aspects that make up your life, how you currently feel about them and their importance to you, for your BestLife now and for your future BestLife.

You may be unaware of how you have stopped activities you previously loved or stopped dreaming about your future. You may already have a bucket list of things you'd like to do someday, but have no idea how that fits in with you and your life right now. This chapter will bring these to the forefront of your conscious mind so that you can choose where you want to spend your time and energy, and what you can't wait for the future to be best for you.

It is super important to your success at establishing your BestLife to know where you are coming from, where you are now and where you are going. Without this knowledge, you don't have your things to choose from. You don't know what you don't know and how the impact of decisions made in the past are influencing your current and future life. The impact of past decisions on the actions you are currently taking is in your subconscious mind. That impact is currently guiding your actions via your reptilian brain having decided what is "safe" and what is not.

You need to assess where you are now and where you have come from because you can only change what you are aware of in your conscious mind. You need to evaluate and undo the subconscious programming of patterns that do not serve you and that you are continuing to repeat.

You will look at how the experiences have shaped who you are today.

Without bringing the past into your current timeline, you don't know how it is affecting you. This part will show you how to consciously bring the past into your awareness. By looking at the stories you tell yourself, you can learn the impact of the past on your current actions.

Throughout your life, various aspects have been important, and the values associated with certain parts of life have also changed. You can learn a lot about why you are living the life you currently live from your past experiences of the different stages. You can also learn a great deal about your current and future BestLife by examining each aspect of your current life and assessing how happy or unhappy you are with it.

Your Past Life

The stages of life have the greatest influence on us. They are formed via the natural order of things: being born, surviving, procreating, surviving as long as you can and then dying. But they are also formed by our society and the accepted conventions for the areas we move in: education, marriage, wealth, religion, manners and authority. So much external influence can mean you make choices that may be perceived as safe because they are what is expected of you. A lot of the values and beliefs that you hold about yourself come from past experiences and interactions with others, and the choices that you made for and about yourself because of those influences.

It works like this: You have an experience. The reptilian brain then files that experience against its safety filter. Did this experience make me feel safe? Then I want to repeat it. Did it hurt me? Then I must never do it again. Was it difficult? I must proceed with caution next time. The reptilian brain remembers past history and has learned that if the experience was painful, it will hurt us again if we repeat it. So it creates these belief systems that "keep us safe" and stop us from repeating them. Beliefs like "I'm not sporty," or "I'm a rubbish writer" or "I'll never get that job."

These beliefs tend to show up negatively in the way you think, speak and act. They use both your internal voices, especially the Loud Shouty Voice that says, "I'd best not because…" or "I'm not good enough to…."

Because these beliefs are not driven by your conscious thought, you have to do some research. You need to take a quick spin through your life and see what pops up as you consider the past. Most of the aspects that pop up will not be surprising to you, but we need them up in your consciousness for you to decide how they fit into your BestLife. If there is anything traumatic that pops up, I would highly recommend getting professional therapy to help you work through it safely.

The easiest way to discover the impact of past experiences on your current life is to tell the story of a part of your life to someone you trust to listen attentively, or record it for later listening. Make the storytelling as interesting and evocative as possible to hold the listener's interest. The reason is that when we tell stories, it frees us from the restraints of convention and allows our unconscious mind to emerge. Think of dreaming but awake!

When you and your trusted friend review the story told, make sure you listen for the types of language you use. Words are super powerful, so it is worth paying attention to how you hear, think and speak them. Pay attention to how the words make you feel: happy, sad, angry, elated, etc. Then see if that emotion about that experience has affected what you currently feel or do in your life.

For help pinpointing which emotions you're feeling, you can check out the feelings wheel at https://feelingswheel.com.

The Stages of Life (According to Me!)

To help you explore this further, I'm going to go through the stages of life, explain the possible impacts and share with you some stories to illustrate how these experiences have had an impact, to a greater or lesser extent, on my current life.

0 to 10: The Early Years

As kids, our priority is to play, have fun, make friends and laugh; be silly and not take anything too seriously. There is a large emphasis, from adults, on learning all sorts of things, but ask any child and they are unlikely to say their top fun thing is to sit in a classroom, tidy their room or eat their vegetables!

The largest impact on their immediate BestLife is the learning and behaviour, and this is where the natural, innate desire to enjoy life starts to morph and conform to the expectations of others. Innate interests, such as a love of nature, painting or taking things apart and trying to put them back together, can manifest as individual traits.

Some families will often notice these traits and encourage their children towards these areas because they want their kids to be happy. Some families will ignore these traits and perhaps encourage their children to pursue areas that they, themselves, have found interesting or useful in their own lives. Adults with authority, especially within learning environments, also have a huge impact on what children do, for good or bad, and everything in between.

From a very early age, I loved lasagne and hated shellfish. I still love lasagne and hate shellfish. My mother taught me how to make lasagne her way (still the best way), and this is how I still make lasagne. No other lasagne has ever been as good. I associate the smells and taste of this lasagne with the ritual afternoon of making it together, building it step by step in the warm, cosy kitchen. It is a past experience that I still create to embody those same feelings, even though my mother is no longer with me. It is an experience that I choose to continue, to connect my past with my present and my future. Both my adult children have been known to be tempted back home with the prospect of homemade lasagne!

My mother also had a strict policy that we taste all new foods we come across and regularly retaste those we don't like. I discovered very early (about 7 years old) that shellfish were the food of the devil. Unfortunately, everyone else in the family loved it. So I had to keep trying it. Now I choose to avoid it at all costs as I have a visceral reaction at the thought of eating it. I also decided that although I agreed with my mother's thoughts that new things are there to be experienced, I would never force my children to experience them if they didn't want to and certainly not make them repeat the experience over and over.

Also, from a very early age, I loved to sing and dance. In the 1970s, when I was growing up in primary school, I participated in pantos and took ballet classes from the age of 2 1/2 to 9 years old. Dancing and singing were a huge passion and part of who I was as a happy kid.

When it came to choosing my secondary school, I wanted to attend a ballet school, but my ballet teacher advised me not to bother. She said I was the wrong shape and would never make it, so I need not apply. I didn't dance again in any performance capacity until my late 30s! This teacher's opinion formed the basis not only for the choices I made in my hobbies but also an internal belief that my body shape was wrong. The awareness of this experience, combined with a 1970s/1980s-style upbringing and comments I received as a child, has had a resonating impact on my life as an adult. It wasn't until I started looking at my filters and values, as well as my past and present experiences, that I could see the limitation I had put on myself and was able to change it to serve me better.

11 to 18: The Teenage Years

At this stage, learning about society and responsibilities begins to affect emotional and mental health. Physical changes also affect all aspects of life in both good and bad ways.

Your BestLife: Past, Present and Future

There is an external pressure to fit in, do what is expected at the time it is expected, and for the future. All at a time when the hormones are raging and the very essence of being a teenager is to rebel and push the boundaries.

The BestLife for teenagers can look like independence from their elders and experimentation with things that aren't allowed. As personalities start to develop, so too does the need to explore. Certain aspects for individuals start to become important: a creative or artistic streak, a fascination with how things are made, a love of crowds, hobbies start to really be explored and friendships become a make-or-break of our day-to-day happiness.

It is at this time of life that the external pressure questions start being asked:

What do you want to be when you grow up?

What are you good at?

What university will you go to?

What will you study?

You are expected to know the answers, and if you don't, an adult in authority may tell you what they think you should do.

As a teenager in the 1980s, I wanted to be a fighter pilot, but I was told that girls were not allowed. The careers teacher at school said I could always consider a career in air traffic control instead. I remember thinking, "Absolutely no way!" I knew then that watching others live the life I wanted to live would bring me great misery.

I also never fit in with the "cool" or the "clever" crowd and spent a lot of time trying to. I felt I was on the outside of the fun life, looking in. Life felt much happier once I discovered cider and boys, but that came with its own dramas.

Academically, I was incredibly bright but not clever at exams, and the studying required for external success measurements. I now had no idea what I wanted to do when I grew up. My careers teacher told me not to bother going to university as I would never make anything of myself. Combine that with a health check nurse, who, in front of the whole class, measured me and said I was as wide as I was tall. I left this phase of life with more than a few untrue beliefs in myself: I was thick, I wouldn't make anything of myself, I was the wrong shape and I would never be part of the in crowd. I already had "proof" from my 0 to 10 years that I was the wrong shape. These experiences cemented those beliefs internally.

It took a lot of work and time to process these damaging beliefs, especially on my own. And it is still an ongoing story for me for some of it. But knowing what the story was, I have been able to consciously make decisions that best supported me as I grew up in my life. And all of it has led me here to this place, writing this book and living my BestLife.

19 to 25: The Young Adult Years

This stage is made for exploring all aspects of life. The world is your oyster! The choice is yours! Learning how you want to be and how you want to live. Living independently from family and making great and not-so-great decisions. Often, the only limiting factor is money, which can be a good and a bad thing! It can be exciting, scary or both at the same time.

Often, it is a time of extremes. On the one hand, going to university or college, starting employment so you can live independently, settling down with a partner and starting on the accepted path of growing up, getting a home, getting married. On the other hand, working several jobs for short periods allows you to travel the world with no commitments and no worries.

In an ideal world, this would be the perfect time to start practising living your best life. In the past, there has been little emphasis on living well and the personal skills necessary to live well on one's own terms. It is only recently, from 2020 during the COVID years, that there has been an opportunity to reflect on the quality of life we live and how we can change it for the better.

My personal story for this time had me trying to prove my career teacher wrong by attending university, and failing. I lasted six months before I realised it wasn't for me. That led me to try many different jobs and careers to find the thing that floated my boat. I also felt a lot of pressure to find a decent job and settle down. I was living very conventionally, with occasional bouts of breaking free, before succumbing to behaving and living in the way I "should." It was this time in my life that I survived a destructive, mentally abusive relationship; I had stayed in it due to the previous stages of my life when I was told I wasn't good enough and would never find anyone else.

Fortunately, one of my breaking-free episodes lasted longer, and I was able to see the wood for the trees. I found space to evaluate my life and how happy (or not) I was. It was a rare opportunity to change my personal direction, which I seized instantly. It is often the case that change in our lives only happens when we hit rock bottom.

Although the story has a happy ending, in that I was out of an unhappy relationship, I was left with more beliefs about myself that shaped how I lived moving forward – the main one being that I wasn't good enough and a failure.

26 to 35: The Settling Down Years

Culture and biology define this time when we settle down and make our own families. It used to be buying a home, getting married and having kids. Now it is less definitive. But the pull to create the family unit is at its greatest here. Most people choose this scenario, whether through conscious or unconscious thought. Often, external pressure from family can sway you in one direction or another. It can feel like a choice you must make rather than one you want to choose. The decisions you make can feel like a series of involuntary turnings leading you down a road you weren't expecting. The path can feel harder to change the further along the road you go. It can feel lucky if the decision you make leaves you feeling happy, secure and moving forward in alignment with your beliefs or unlucky, but not much you can do if it doesn't feel this way!

I worked with an individual who had reached this particular stage of life. They had ticked all the conventional boxes: becoming a fully qualified professional, living with a less-than-supportive partner and working for a less-than-supportive boss. They were feeling like they were failing in life. Their story is theirs to tell, but when I listened to how they told the stories of their life, it was clear that self-worth, or the lack of it, was a core foundation built on very rocky ground. They did not feel like they were worth spending time on or with, and because of that, they surrounded themselves with people who also supported this belief.

Once we spent time working together to rebuild their foundation, they began to believe that they *were* worth spending time with and *were* worth investing in themselves to make the changes they identified to improve their life. Small positive actions began to emerge, followed by slightly larger and bolder ones. Shortly afterwards, the nonsupportive partner and the nonsupportive boss were no longer in their life. By examining the past story, they liberated themselves from past actions and were able to choose a new foundational belief and a new story to tell. As a result, they are now living their best life on their terms.

36 to 45: The Early Midlife Years

A time of stability for most, whether that is by choice or by need or by convention. Careers, family life choices, friendships and community tend to be established and stable. The words routine and familiar are used to describe this stage of life. Work demands, children and commitments mean that the fun stuff often gets dropped off the list. You're so busy living the life you have that you don't have time, energy or inclination to think about the life you want…unless something goes awry.

This is the stage at which many people tend to overlook their own well-being. Looking after and supporting others at work and at home, there seems to be no time for yourself. Compromises are then made without thinking, actions stopped or dropped without regard for the impact on your happiness. Often, changes are made for the greater good of those around you, but to your detriment.

This is where the seeds of sadness, dissatisfaction, depression and unhappiness settle within the mind and body. They're so tiny you barely notice they are there. It feels selfish to put yourself first; other people's needs, wants and demands come first. And often you feel happy to make those choices. And unless the status quo changes, you will continue to do the same as you have always done.

One client I worked with came to me, precisely because this was happening. She came to me to help get herself back on track. She felt she had lost control of her health at this stage in her life. She was essentially living to serve others and had lost herself.

By telling and listening to her stories from the past, she realised how different her upbringing had been and how it had shaped her values. She had chosen the path of partner, home and baby: They had moved out to the country from city life. She worked school hours and after-bedtime hours so that she could be a mum first, but also maintain her career, which was important for her identity as well as for their financial stability. Listening to her story, it was clear their relationship was full of love, compromise and communication, but their values were not aligned. Before having children, the value mismatch was not high on my priority list in life, and it didn't seem like a big deal. But once the pressures of bringing up a child together were combined with the values mismatch, it turned into a large issue. Neither of them was prepared to compromise on what that life looked like for them in the present, which meant that after relationship counselling, they decided to go their separate ways, but with a strong foundation to co-parent with love.

I worked with my client through this process, supporting, listening and guiding her through her journey back to herself. Her belief that it's possible to stay true to her values, nurture herself, and reclaim her health has helped her maintain the internal resilience and clarity that living her BestLife is vital to her whole family unit, rather than stagnating and suffocating under someone else's belief system.

46 to 65: The Later Midlife

Also known as the "sandwich generation," which refers to adults who are caring for both children and parents. This is when the elders and youngsters of the family place demands that are often out of your control. As much as the Early Midlife years are often about stability around your life choices with all the pulls on your time, the Later Midlife years can feel like a magnified version of what has gone before, and with fewer choices around your actions.

It is often a stage when your physicality can start to play tricks on you, with injuries occurring, hormonal changes that are beyond our control and our metabolism slowing down at the same time we become less active. In addition, hormonal changes affect our mental and emotional health with a variety of different impacts that vary from person to person.

These physical changes, combined with the mental and emotional changes, can affect you and everything around you. How do you see yourself as an individual and in relation to others in your circles? Add to this the external influences of ageing within work environments, the pull of teenage and adult children, as well as parents with deteriorating health, and it can feel like your life is not your own. You are no longer choosing your own life path but are at the beck and call of your loved ones.

A client of mine in their late 50s has lived with the pull of her family for years. While running her own business, she would regularly adjust her work plans to accommodate her adult children and elderly parents. She came to me because she recognised that, in order to live well, she needed to prioritise herself so she could be in the best place to support her loved ones whilst continuing to run her successful business.

Through the stories she told about past events, we established that she had a need to be needed and had actively trained her family to ask for her help, even on small issues, because her value was being needed to help her feel loved. She *did* feel loved and valued, but she was drowning under the demands on her time, and it was affecting her physical, mental and emotional health. It was also starting to make her feel resentful towards her loved ones, as she was having to put her business on hold more and more.

Left unchanged, the consequences could have been burnout for her or ruined family relationships due to conflicting communications and a lack of understanding of each individual's needs and expectations between family members.

We worked on the stories she had been telling herself and the beliefs and language she had been using. We gradually changed the narrative around her values and how she presented herself to her family. Once some boundaries around self-care and work were established and communicated to the family, she was in a better position to consider the choices she wanted to make about moving forward in her life and what her core values and priorities were. She now measures actions against those values and priorities, and makes choices accordingly. She is living her BestLife, with the flexibility to respond to the needs of her loved ones.

66 to 100+: The Wise Years

I never know what label sits well with me when describing this stage of life, as it can be so different for each and every one of us. I'm going to call them the "wise years." It is at this stage in life that it is commonplace for you to look back on your life and decide what you did well and not so well. At the beginning of this stage, there is often a feeling of liberation and a mindset of "Why not?" A new sense of potential opens up once the work is done and the kids are grown. Anything is possible. You don't feel old, but outside influences start to refer to you as old.

As this stage goes on, you start feeling the external influences. In culture, you are both venerated and ignored, respected and invisible, valued but an inconvenience. It is a time when you often have great health and can choose to go on adventures you couldn't when you were committed in previous stages of life. Or you are unlucky and your body decides to make you live a life you didn't choose. Or you experience both. It almost seems like Russian roulette.

It's a time you want to spend with family, but you're also aware that you may be affecting how they live. It is a time when nature encourages you to look forward to the end of life and consider how that might unfold, as well

Your BestLife: Past, Present and Future

as how it could be. It is a natural time of evaluation and consolidation of knowledge, experiences, and hopefully a life well-lived. A time when the words "I lived my BestLife," "I am happy," "I wish…" or "I regret not doing…" start to resonate.

One of the important aspects I have found, when working with individuals at this stage, is to listen carefully to the stories they tell. They reverberate with emotion that will influence how they live these years. One individual said they never shared their health concerns with their family as they did not want them worrying about things they couldn't change. However, upon listening to them, it became clear that by not sharing, they were undermining the trust and closeness of those family relationships. The individual had stopped visiting family and changed plans when hospital appointments were happening. And because they were withdrawing their time, the family felt the absence. Had this behaviour been left to continue, the feeling of estrangement from the family could have increased and become irreparable. Once my client saw the impact of not sharing, even though it came from a well-meaning place, they were able to reconnect with their family and invite their support. As a result, they felt able to share and involve their family – a family that wanted to know and discuss plans for the future so they could all share and live together again.

A Life Well-Lived From Beginning to End

Living your life well is living your BestLife. Part of that is looking back and evaluating the impact events have had on your life, accepting the beliefs and aspects you want to continue living with and changing those aspects you are not prepared to live by.

By looking at the stage of life you are currently at, you can clearly see the impact you currently have on your life and the internal and external influences on it.

If you don't regularly take time to reflect on where you have come from, what you have been doing and the consequences of those actions, you may not realise the impact, both internally and externally, until you are on a path you did not choose. By then, finding your way back to your best life can be much harder.

It is your choice and your responsibility to continually look back from where you have come and look forward to where you want to go, whilst ensuring that your "right now" is constantly the best version for you.

Exercise: Story Time

In this exercise, you are going to tell the stories of your life. For each stage, there will be dominant experiences and moments that have helped define who you are now. By examining those events through stories, you can bring to your conscious mind the values, beliefs and lessons you have learned, and be able to choose which you will take forward into your BestLife.

Look Back

Go through each of the stages of life up to now and tell yourself your story of each stage.

Write it down, speak it, record it, whatever works for you.

Listen to the emotions and language you use.

Ask yourself the questions:

> What emotions are staying with me from that story?
>
> What is the impact on me of that story?
>
> How can I use that story to make my current life better?

Look Forward

Look at each of the stages you are yet to live and tell yourself a story of the future you. Again, listen to the emotions and language you use.

Ask yourself the questions:

> What emotions are staying with me from that story?
>
> What is the impact on me of that story?
>
> How can I use that story to make my current life better?

Story of Today

Now look at the life you are living right now. Tell the story of how it works and feels. Your highs and lows and the impact of your current decisions on your happiness and ability to lead your BestLife.

And ask:

> What needs to change?
>
> What am I happy with?
>
> What do I not want to continue to do?

In summary, by looking back at where you have come from and reviewing past decisions and actions, you can course-correct your road into the future. Your ability to review, reset and route plan your best direction makes the difference between your average or worse life and your BestLife.

Your BestLife: What Does It Look Like?

In this section, we are going to talk about our Lost and Founds, our Hopes and Dreams.

For clarity, if we don't evaluate what we have lost, what we have stopped doing and why we stopped, then our choice is removed from us. And if we don't give space for our hopes and dreams for the future, then we cannot learn new things, challenge ourselves and grow as individuals. Ultimately, without looking at what we have lost and what we could gain, we will end up living inside the reptilian comfort box of neither thriving nor living our BestLife.

As you grow up and live life, at no point are you taught to continue dreaming, imagining or evaluating how much you are actively enjoying your life. You're not taught that regularly making the course corrections needed to keep enjoying life is what allows you to live your BestLife consistently.

The default setting amongst most adults, especially in the early to late midlife years, is to just continue plodding on – not actually choosing what happens but reacting to external influences and swallowing down any misgivings about wasting time. Living life by reacting as your default doesn't lead to a BestLife for you. Acting with knowledge and making regular choices means that the balance between the stuff you have to do and the stuff you want to do works in your favour and not against you.

And when you do more of the stuff you want to do, you are happier in body, mind and soul. When you are happier in body, mind and soul, you look at life through the positive eyes of possibility rather than the negative eyes of duty and sacrifice.

So let's take that time now to examine what, in an ideal world, your BestLife would include.

As you travel through the various stages of life, different aspects of your life change in priority. So it's really important when you're looking at living your best life that

Your BestLife: What Does It Look Like?

you constantly assess where you are in relation to those aspects that are important to you.

Having a running list of those aspects can help ease the transition between one life stage and another. By selecting your focus and knowing which aspects you are setting aside in favour of others, it helps the brain feel safe and secure even when change is happening. Knowing that anything you set aside will not be lost in the ether of living life – and that you can evaluate it and bring it back into your BestLife when you are ready – can be incredibly reassuring.

For example, I worked with a fabulous client who ran her own business and also loved to run long distances. The time commitment of both these aspects was large, as was the physical and mental resilience required for both. This was all well and good whilst her home life was stable with a supportive partner and a teenage child. When other parts of her life started to creep in and affect her ability to maintain these two important aspects, her mental and emotional health was significantly affected, and her life became less than enjoyable.

She felt pulled in several different directions, her emotions swinging from overwhelming to feeling like a failure to exhaustion. Emotional burnout was definitely in the future if nothing changed. Her compromise at the time meant she had to reduce her hours at work and drastically cut back on running to almost nothing, in order to make space for the new aspects of her life. But this left her without the ability to fuel her emotional resilience, and her capacity to thrive was almost non-existent.

By working with my client to examine *all* aspects of her life – the good, the bad, the ugly and the indifferent – as they stood, and by looking at both her past and future to spot anything that could affect her ability to live her BestLife moving forward, we were able to build a clear picture of what really mattered. We then sat down and worked through the big list, narrowing it down to the key, high-priority aspects that would keep her in her BestLife over the next six months, while everything else settled down.

The result was a plan of action that incorporated all the important aspects of her life, alongside her current life priorities, which included "adulting" (the tasks we have to do but wouldn't necessarily choose to do). Making a plan and finding a route that she could control and act on gave her back a sense of autonomy and choice in her actions. The route plan helped her regain control of her life and happiness. With that sense of control, she could

Your BestLife: What Does It Look Like?

celebrate the wins and start thriving again. The result? A happy, healthy client who was able to do the adulting tasks without sacrificing her BestLife!

So let's take this time to make a list of the things you love and that are important and valued to you, things that have gotten away because life got *in* the way: hobbies you no longer do but would like to do again, experiences you would like to have but haven't yet had.

We are going to now look at your life from Now to Z. Anything is possible. Are you excited? Are you ready? This is going to be a quick-fire brain dump, your opportunity to get everything out of your head that could possibly float your boat in life.

Lost and Found

First stop: looking at the things you used to do that you have lost in your life, and that you'd like to do again.

The whole idea, when looking at your BestLife is, it's got to excite you, it's got to float your boat. It's got to make you go, "Hell yeah, I'm prepared to do stuff to get this result!"

For example, I want to help more people. I can only support so many one-to-one clients in the shed. But one of the things that floats my boat, as we know it's my core value, is leaving everyone better off than when I found them. The more people I help, the more I fulfil my purpose: to change the world, one person at a time. Because every time I help someone thrive, they are better equipped to put their magic out in the world. Living their BestLife brings joy, which then helps those around them. And those people will, in turn, be better able to serve others. That ripple of positive change continues, changing the world, one person at a time. Even helping someone a tiny bit can make a real difference.

I used to do this by running my Superstar Groups and 1:1 sessions from the Shed of Strength. These were magical 60- to 90-minute sessions a week for individuals to spend time building themselves up physically, mentally and emotionally. I stopped running these groups in 2020 when COVID hit, as face-to-face groups were not allowed. I took the groups online for the duration of the COVID lockdowns. But when we were all released back into the social wild, the world had changed, and the groups no longer worked. So I have reworked The Southey Way so that I can help more people.

I lost the amazing Superstars group. However, by examining what I had lost and why I had loved it, I was able to find a new approach to achieve the same Superstar Group vibes and results. By taking the new version online, I have opened up the opportunity to help even more people. By losing one thing, I was able to reset and discover something even better.

It's the way that I've made it work for me to achieve what I want to achieve. I *love* doing my one-to-ones in the shed. I'm never going to give that up. But helping others find their way to living their BestLife, I have created opportunities to help more people and have greater fulfilment within my life.

Hopes and Dreams

Once you have looked at your Lost and Found, you can open the doors to your Hopes and Dreams.

Between Now and Z, what's on your bucket list? If you could do anything at all, no questions asked, no restrictions, what would it be?

For me, my dream is to travel independently more and really explore and experience different cultures, countries and people. Currently, the dream looks like it is more off-roading in our truck, being self-sufficient with minimal "stuff" – just the bare minimum with no external agendas.

Travelling to all the countries, but never on a package tour, is a significant driver for me.

Money on its own doesn't matter to me, but being able to do those trips does, so money figures in attaining my hopes and dreams. So, being able to finance the trips and having my successful, purpose-driven, heart-led business are key components of that dream.

Your hopes and dreams need to be explored so you can determine when they may come true and what steps you need to take to make them a reality. If you don't dream, you cannot create a plan to actually achieve them!

So what are your Lost and Founds and Hopes and Dreams? What experiences have you had or want? What do they look like? Where do you want your next stage in life to take you? It could be anything. This is your pie in the sky, anything is possible, dream-big kind of thinking.

Exercise: Lost and Found and Hopes and Dreams

By the end of this exercise, you could be buzzing about your potential. Your BestLife right there on paper to be implemented by you! Exciting stuff!

It is also entirely possible that at the end of this exercise, you will be feeling overwhelmed or sad. That is completely normal, too.

Often, when you know you are not happy and you look at your life and all the things you could be or do, the emotions will be running high. They don't have to be all positive, but they do need to be out there in the open for you to see.

Fear not. You have to review the route already taken and the destinations you want to visit before you can plan the best route to take. The next stages in this book will help you build your BestLife plan so you can know what life you want to live, create the plan and with each step move towards your ultimate BestLife. Knowing that with each step, you are living the life you want to live.

Know that you can be multiple versions of the same person. They all exist within you, and you choose when or whether they will emerge into the light of life. There is no right or wrong to living your best life. If you are living it and you are happy, then that is exactly where you need to be at that point.

This exercise is to get all your Losts and Founds, Hopes and Dreams out of your heart and head and into the open. By throwing them into the light, your conscious mind will be able to decide which are vital for your BestLife and which are not currently high priority. Then you will be able to create a picture of your journey and the destinations you want to get to at this point in your life.

This will be your starting list to work from when making the RoadMap to your BestLife.

Lost and Found

Let's find out what you've stopped doing; maybe you'd like to start again, and what you're still doing that you no longer want to do.

By answering the next set of questions, you will get more clarity on both the stop and the start and begin to imagine what the future would be like if you lived more of your dreams.

What did you used to do that you loved?

What do you do now that you love?

What would you love to do in the future?

What really floats your boat about your life?

If you could do anything, live any way, what would that look like?

What is stopping you from doing the things you love that you listed above?

What action would encourage you to *do* one of the things you love?

What have you done in the past that you disliked?

What are you doing currently that you dislike?

What in your future life looks like no fun?

What are you holding on to or doing just because you think you "should"?

Why do you choose to do something you dislike?

What action would encourage you to *stop* doing one of the things you love?

Hopes and Dreams

Ask yourself all the following questions and jot down the answers that first pop into your head. Use your answers from the exercises in Parts 1 and 2 as prompts when you get stuck for ideas.

Remember to listen for your Quiet Inner Voice as well as your Loud Shouty voice. Both will give you information that can be used to dream big!

Here are some questions to get you started:

Who are you?

What is important to you

What are your values

What do you love to do?

Where do you love to be?

What are you not prepared to compromise on?

What makes you ecstatically happy or emotional?

Your BestLife: What Does It Look Like?

Where have you got lost on the road?

What have you given up that you'd love to take back up at some time?

What experiences do you want to have in your life journey?

What's important to you?

What do you never want to regret missing?

If you could do/be/live anywhere, where would it be?

Where will your evolving BestLife take you?

If anything were possible, what would your life right now look like?

What are the non-negotiables in your life?

Keep asking yourself questions until your brain, heart and gut are empty of ideas.

Summary

Looking at your answers to the questions for Lost and Found and Hopes and Dreams, write yourself a statement to answer each of the two following questions:

What would your BestLife feel and look like?

What would your Shit Life feel and look like to you?

Part 2: Now to Z Wrap-Up

To summarise the section Now to Z, you have looked at:

- ★ Where you are on your A to Z of Life
- ★ The Good, the Bad and the Ugly in your Life
- ★ Your Agenda vs. other people's
- ★ The internal dialogue between your Two Voices
- ★ How you see yourself
- ★ How to spot your filters
- ★ The stories from your stages of life
- ★ Your lost and founds, your hopes and dreams

The exercises you have completed will have given you a whole load of information on where you currently are and where you want to go. Each of these is essential to consider when looking at where you want to go next.

Let's create your Destination Summary so you have a point of reference to check in on as you make your plan and take those next steps.

Exercise: Destination Summary

The combination of these with your summary sheet from the previous section A to Now will provide the foundation for your next stage: Route Planning. The time is now to create your route for your BetLife RoadMap.

On a new sheet of paper, write today's date. You are going to summarise the key points of Part 2: Now to Z.

From Exercise: Where are You?

Where are you currently on your journey through the A to Z of Life?

What is the scale you are measuring against?

From Exercise: Good, Bad and Ugly

What is the best thing on your Good List that you would love to keep doing?

What is the worst thing on your Bad list that you want to stop doing ASAP?

What is the ugliest thing on your ugly list that you can't not do but needs to change to work better for you?

From Exercise: Create and Keep Your Agenda

What is the most valuable Agenda item to you right now?

What difference will it make in your life?

From Exercise: Find Your Filters

What filter did you discover that surprised you?

What filter did you discover that you want to change immediately?

From Exercise: Story Time

Which stage of life do you currently resonate with?

Which story of your life stages did you find easiest to tell?

Which story of your life stages did you find the hardest to tell?

What did you discover?

From Exercise: Lost and Found, Hopes and Dreams

What did you lose but want back in your life in some way?

What are your hopes and dreams for the future?

Now to Z Wrap-Up

Congratulations! You now have two summaries: The RoadMarker summary of where you are right now and the Destination summary of where you want to go next.

So let's go! Your next steps are to navigate your route and start creating your RoadMap for your next BestLife.

Part 3:

Your BestLife RoadMap

Roadmap: Route Planning

It is time to create your BestLife RoadMap.

In Parts 1 and 2, you looked at:

A to Now - where you have come from, who you currently are and how you are currently living

Now to Z - who you are, your stories and filters and your Hopes and Dreams combined with your Lost and Founds

Now, you are in the best position to start creating your BestLife RoadMap.

We start Part 3 with Route Planning: mapping out what you want and where you want to start heading in your life. A life of Purpose, focus and happiness, chosen and led by you. This is your time to look at your Destination: where you want to go and choose the cities/towns/villages and countryside you want to visit along the way!

It is time to sort through all the thoughts and ideas you have put on paper and decide which you want to action NOW in your route plan, which you want to action at a later date and which you can put in a route planner folder for the next time you complete your Best Life RoadMap.

As discussed in Parts 1 and 2, the reptilian brain fears change and will throw up roadblocks to keep you from continuing down the road. If you can build a strong case for moving forward, one that feels more appealing than staying where you are, then the reptilian brain is less likely to throw up disruptions. And the smaller the changes you make, the less fearful the brain will be.

So in this Part 3, we shall look at how to narrow down the changes you want to make and the actions you want to take. Then, we'll break down those actions into the smallest possible steps whilst also building a positive picture of change, one that reassures the brain that this new action is safe and not a threat.

From this point, you are going to work through all the exercises that you've done in Part 1 and your RoadMarker Summary, and the exercises in Part 2 with your Destination

RoadMap: Route Planning

Summary. You're going to consolidate them all and write about where you want to go and how you plan to get there. This is called Route Planning.

In Parts 1 and 2, you have literally dumped everything from your brain onto the table. Now, you will choose what to focus on. It is important to maintain a focus, as your effort and energy will be directed wherever you direct your attention.

Remember: Energy flows where your focus goes.

It is always you, as the individual, who chooses what to focus on, because you need to take ownership of your choices and actions. Your brain also needs to be on board with the changes you are about to make.

This book helps you create your plan and find ways to make your plan work. What you then have to do is implement your plan. A key and vital part of the SOS Life Academy is creating regular space for you to work *on* your life, rather than constantly being caught up *in* it. It's about taking space *out* of your life so you can focus *on* it.

For your BestLife RoadMap to be successful, you have to build in regular check-ins to ensure you are still on the right path. When something resonates, that's your cue to take action.

If you are one of the world's readers and not doers, this book will not work at its best for you. Without action, your life will not change for the better. If you don't act on the changes you decide on after working with this book, then your brain will resist future changes even more. Your subconscious needs to believe you will follow through to create new, sustainable habits.

If you definitely want to live your BestLife, then now is the time to commit to building your full picture RoadMap. This is the work that will convince your brain you are serious about taking action. When you commit to and take action consistently, you are proving to your reptilian brain that implementing your BestLife RoadMap leads to greater things and even better safety.

Part of my best life is these huge off-roading trips I take with my husband and kids. Taking a big chunk of time out of my working life to do and experience different things in the world. I particularly loved the Sahara Desert because it wasn't about people, places or tourist routes. It was about space and the vast expanse of time, as revealed in the fossilised coral in the middle of the desert, the cave paintings and etchings from long ago, when hunters watched for food by the side of now non-existent rivers. There was space to think and be free in your thinking. And for me, it was one of the most special trips I've ever done. I want more of these trips to become a regular part of my life. Adventures off the beaten track, which not many have a chance to experience, fill my soul and help me frame my life in the world. This way, I am better able to help others with an open mind.

So I have committed to a route of action that will lead me to experience more adventurous trips like this one. My personal RoadMap includes small steps that remind me of the special feelings of being out on these trips. These small steps constantly reassure my reptilian brain that it is a necessary part of keeping me safe and making sure all three of my Levels of Living are kept fulfilled.

Traffic Lights

In Part 3, the Route Planning stage, you are going to look at those exercises you did in Parts 1 and 2 and "traffic-light" them.

Traffic lights are an accepted part of our culture and an easy way to categorise all those items we want to *go* ahead with (Green), *stop* doing altogether (Red) and *prepare/ consider* whether to continue (Amber).

You're then going to act on the greens and cut out of your life any reds that you can possibly cut out. What you will be left with is all your ambers. Those items that need to adapt, change or be paused for a while so that they work better for you.

Traffic-lighting your life can be fun. It's an opportunity to feel what life could be like without all the shit bits and using your time and energy on all the fun, worthwhile and useful bits! The Brain Dump Mind Map exercise you completed in Part 1 is going to make traffic-lighting your life super easy. Because if you've mind mapped this onto a piece of paper, you can literally get your coloured pencils and go with your Inner Quiet Voice to find the truth!

Exercise: Traffic-Light Your Life

Get yourself red, orange and green pens or pencils. I like traffic light colours because we've been trained on what they mean.

Red = STOP

Green = GO

Amber = Proceed with CAUTION

Pull up your Brain Dump Mind Map Exercise in front of you and look at each item you have written on your smiley face map.

You are going to get circling!

You are going to draw circles around your Mind Dump items, separating them into categories: Go/Stop/Proceed with Caution.

Green = Go

We will start with the easy ones. The ones that you want to carry on doing with no change.

Start with your green pen for your Green Traffic Light.

Green is for GO – all the things you still want to do with no alteration. Circle in green all the things that are absolutely hunky dory, that you will continue to do, that you don't need to or want to change.

Red = Stop

Now look at those items you don't want to do. Don't worry about how that will happen yet. In your future BestLife, these items would not be done by you.

Red is for STOP – all the things you have a choice over that you don't want to do anymore. Circle in red anything you don't want to do anymore; the stuff you hate, that fills you with dread.

A note: There are always going to be items that we don't want to do but have to do in life. These are not your red lights. You are looking for the items that you don't *want* to do. If you are not sure whether an item is a Red, ask yourself: Can you delegate? Can you get rid of it? Can somebody else do it? And if you were stuck in bed for five days, would anything fall apart if it didn't get done?

For example, I absolutely loathe cleaning and don't want to do it, but I could get someone else to do it for me, so it is a red for me. Paying my mortgage is something I really

RoadMap: Route Planning

don't like doing, but it has to happen and is nobody else's responsibility. So it's an amber, not a red.

Amber = Proceed with Caution

Once you've circled all of your greens and reds, you will be left with uncircled items: These are the ambers.

Amber is the adulting stuff you have to keep doing, but it's about finding a way to make it work better for you, or seeking help or assistance to make it more acceptable to you.

Ambers need considering, reframing, repurposing and rewarding.

Something needs to change with your ambers to bring them closer to a green and further away from a red. Go ahead and circle all the ambers.

At this point, you may find yourself second-guessing your colour choices, often between the reds and ambers. If in doubt, make it amber.

Once you have completed traffic-lighting your life, you will have a colour-coded piece of paper. There may be a dominant colour. You can use that awareness as a quick measure for your current BestLife, a little bit of potential learning right there. If there are a lot of reds and/or a lot of ambers, that is a clear indication that life could be a lot better for you once you take control of those items.

What does *your* map look like?

What is the dominant colour?

How does the balance of the three colours make you feel??

What amber or red tasks could you say *no* to doing right now?

One Thing

What one thing from your Red will you drop right now?

Why will that benefit you and your BestLife?

Bonus Time

What one item can you change now to get more green? Once you've thought about it, choose another item to action. Repeat until the balance of your traffic lights is working in your favour more often than not!

Roadmap: Choosing Your Route

The next part of the RoadMap planning is to look at your ambers from your Brain Dump Mind Map: Things that you have to do that still have to be part of your life, but could be changed, tweaked or reframed to come closer to green than red in your life.

Pick one to three of the ambers to focus on reframing at this time, because you can't work on all of them all at once. If you've got eight ambers on your list to change, your reptilian brain is going to rebel. It's not going to like changing eight things.

You are just marking the things that are most important *currently*. By changing how they work for you, you will make an immediate big difference in your BestLife, and it is going to raise that item from an amber to closer to a green.

You should now have in front of you the various aspects of your life:

Part 1 - Your journey from A to Now

Part 2 - Your journey from Now to Z

Along with the following exercises:

- ★ RoadMarker Summary
- ★ Destination Summary
- ★ Good, Bad and Ugly
- ★ Lost and Found
- ★ Hopes and Dreams
- ★ Brain Dump MindMap exercise with Red/Amber/Green
- ★ Scores on the Doors

You are in charge of the route that you take from here, and that route is going to be guided by your traffic lights. Where you put your attention is what's most likely to happen. Revisit the exercises from Part 1 and Part 2, and

Roadmap: Choosing Your Route

choose one to three things in your life to focus on now. You now have a wealth of information about yourself – the contents of your brain and what life means to you – laid out on the paper in front of you.

It is time to sort through the brain muddle and identify what you want to focus on now and going forward. Consider short-, medium-, and long-term items.

Pick fun things.

Pick the things you want to change

Pick the non-negotiables.

Perhaps you want to focus on one area, such as how much someone else takes up your time; that alone could be something to work on. Or maybe you have written down travelling the length of the Americas in 2030 as part of your hopes and dreams; add that to your focus list too.

What you focus on is what you will move towards doing. But you can't do anything and everything; the brain will just feel overwhelmed.

Out of all the ideas from inside your head that you have put down on your RoadMarker and Destination summaries, just pick the actions that you are currently going to focus on. These can be a combination of short, medium and long-term focus items. Maybe something from the 3 Levels of Life, something from your Traffic Lights and something from your Destination Summary. Or your one thing could be a theme to focus on, with your one to three things aligning with that.

It doesn't mean you don't do any of the others. It simply means focusing on these things first. You can come back to your notes and choose another focus next time you review your BestLife RoadMap.

For example, in 2024, I was focused on writing this book. Now, writing a book was a huge project that had been on my Hopes and Dreams list since I started my business in 2016. However, I had no idea in 2016 what it would look like or how it would unfold. Fast forward to 2024, and I had a proven track record for delivering my RoadMap, helping my clients create a version that works for them and supporting them whilst they travelled down their road.

So when I did my End of 2024 BestLife Review, I knew it was the right time to focus on getting the book out into the world. At that point, I hadn't written any of it down. The Book felt like a huge and overwhelming task once I had selected it to be my focus.

Roadmap: Choosing Your Route

To help me focus on creating my book, I listed some items that would be challenges to writing the book and some ideas that would help me write the book. I then allowed my brain to be open to finding solutions. Here is my brain dump from my 2024 BestLife RoadMap focus goal of writing the book.

Challenges

As I ran a full-time business alongside my home and family life, I didn't have a lot of spare time. I also have a creative and instinctive brain that allows me to think on my feet, but also that means I'm not much of a systems person or a planner. I struggle to implement consistently without being distracted.

Ideas

How can I get what is in my head into book format without overthinking it?

I love working with people and they help me be my best self. If I can speak it, there must be an app that can transcribe it.

Solutions

Create a workshop that people could attend to experience the structured format of my RoadMap to their BestLife and use it as the foundation of the book.

My 2024 BestLife RoadMap

Theme: SOS your Life: RoadMap to your Bestlife

Timescale: 2025

Main Focus: Write a book that will help as many people as possible take responsibility and action for creating and living their individual Best Lives.

Focus Steps:

1. Run interactive workshops utilising my instinctive creativity, thinking on my feet and delivering my best through engaging with individuals. (Timescale: February 2025)

2. Record the workshops and use an app to transcribe. Use the summary option of the transcribe app to create the headings. (Timescale: March 2025)

3. Using the transcription summary of my workshop as my RoadMap, complete the writing of the book and publish the book *SOS Your Life: RoadMap to your Bestlife*. (Timescale: September 2025)

Above is my version. Yours can look like this or something completely different. The format that my brain works with is going to be different to yours. But the main focus points stay the same. By using the prompts, you will create your own route for your RoadMap.

Now you can decide where you are going to put your focus. Be really clear on how much you want the change you're focusing on, whatever it looks like for you, because the more you want it, the more you're going to enjoy that journey. That desire builds up the anticipation, your vision and your connection to it.

So when you're writing it down, you have to *really want* it. If it doesn't get you excited and chomping at the bit to get stuck in, you don't want it enough yet to counterbalance the reptilian brain's fear of change! Keep writing until you have such a brilliant picture of your future life that you are drawn to action.

If you don't get that feeling, even after all the work, it's not your priority yet. Don't waste your energy on something you don't actually want.

Exercise: Choose Your RoadMap Route

Remember: Our energy flows where our focus goes.

Choose the one, two or three changes that you are going to work on to move down the road to your BestLife. If you are not sure which items to to action, choose one item from each of these categories:

Hopes and Dreams

Lost and Founds

Traffic Lights (pick an amber to turn green)

Make sure you are excited by each item you pick, that you want it and you can see the happiness and fun within it. Most importantly, make sure it aligns with your purpose and values.

Three words of warning:

1. Do not pick too many things to focus on. The more your focus is split and not taking you down the road to your BestLife, the harder and more challenging it will be and the less positive impact it will have on your BestLife.

2. Do not pick something to make others happy if it does not align with you and your BestLife. As

soon as you start being or doing something that you think other people are expecting you to be or do, then you are going against what you truly want. Even if it is with good intentions, it will be harder, feel more draining and not get you where you actually want to go.

3. Remember your pesky prehistoric reptilian brain, in the back there? All it wants from you is not to die. Its only job is to keep you safe, procreate and then not die for as long as possible. That's it. It doesn't care about you being happy. It doesn't want you to do anything different. Because what you have done up until now hasn't killed you. So just keep doing that, and all will be okay. By doing the same as you've always done, you will stay alive. So when you start feeling scared, know that it's just the reptilian brain telling you not to take action.

The action that you want to take has to be more appealing and less dangerous than simply staying where you are.

You have got to *want* what you have chosen with your heart and soul.

Do you want it enough?

RoadMap: Navigating your Route

Everything you are going to go through now to live your BestLife will happen only by doing something different. Your brain will hate it. It's programmed to fear change. You've got to turn your action for change into a big, whopping positive thing. For each focus you choose to action (and again I would only suggest actioning a maximum of three), you need to think of anything that will challenge the actioning and success of this focus and then troubleshoot and find potential solutions.

For each focus you choose, you will need to do the following steps:

- ★ Break down and mark out the smallest steps you need to take to move you towards the end result.

- ★ Be specific on how much you want it and the positive difference it will make in your own life.

- ★ Explore any challenges that you may have or could have that are going to stop it from happening.

- ★ Solution Search against the challenges, so you are prepared for the breakdowns and diversions.

In the previous exercise, you decided where you are going to focus on your current BestLife RoadMap route. Now it's time to troubleshoot. What could go wrong? What will stop you?

Exploring what could go wrong is not negative thinking. It is allowing creative thinking under no pressure. If you have a plan *before* shit hits the fan, you will be less surprised and better prepared to reroute!

For each challenge that comes up in the troubleshooting of your chosen focus, you will need to find at least one solution. When you are travelling on your planned route and that challenge arises, you don't panic and go off on a random detour, because you will already have your planned detour written down.

RoadMap: Navigating Your Route

Without the challenges and solutions done ahead of time, your reptilian brain goes into its fear reactions. You will find yourself carrying out actions that do not support your focus. By completing the challenges and solutions phase, you will be more consistent towards your focus.

Let's look at my 2024 focus on writing this book. You have already seen how I created the RoadMap for it to happen. Next, I completed my Problems and Solutions around it, which looked like this:

Possible Problems

I don't know what I'm doing, having never written a book

What if it's shit?

How do I get it published?

I can't stand mistakes, but how will I spot them?

How will I stay on track whilst still running the business and having a life?

How do I stop the overwhelm and procrastination?

How do I make sure I actually finish and publish the book?

Possible Solutions

Run several workshops and bring the transcriptions together to get a complete picture that I can fill with my voice or writing.

I *do* know what I'm doing, and I have seen my BestLife RoadMap work over and over again. I have the knowledge, the proof and the workshops that will help me get the content out of my head and onto paper.

Investigate options for publishing and follow my Inner Voice to choose the one that will work best for me.

Have someone proofread and edit with fresh eyes.

Have a diary plan around the book deadlines and ensure someone is appointed to hold me accountable.

Break the steps of writing and publishing the book up into the smallest steps and then put them in the work diary to ensure the space is held free to complete them.

Roadmap: Navigating Your Route

Commit to external sources and talk about the finished book, the process and the launch date both to people and on social media.

What I Actually Did

A lot of these possible problems had solutions that could be bundled. When I researched publishers, I found one with an approachable and helpful system that ensured many of my solutions were taken care of under one roof. A schedule of work and actual people to help with book writing, editing, proofreading and accountability, alongside technical details such as layout and graphics, and actual publishing took a lot of the overwhelm away and kept me on track. All that left me focusing on the writing!

Once you have completed your version of this BestLife RoadMap, you will be fully prepared and raring to get on your journey to your BestLife.

Possible Problems and Solutions

Before you get back on the road, you've got time to think through what could go wrong and how you can handle it. By finding possible solutions now, you're better prepared if and when shit hits the fan later on. You will have choices not driven by reaction but by conscious, preplanned thought.

This doesn't mean that you're thinking on the negative side. It just means that you have options readily available: I could do this, or I could do that or I could tweak it this way.

These are the kinds of lists that help your brain accept the change your conscious mind is choosing to make.

Imagine you are literally in your big A to Z road map. You want to go from Plymouth to Carlisle. Same destination, but many different ways to achieve it. You can choose to go on the country roads or the fastest way directly there. You could choose to stop at service stations for a rest or choose to deviate to side towns for a reset.

When planning a trip, there are key aspects: Looking for obstacles and things that can affect our journey. Where's the traffic, where's the roadblocks, where's the accidents? Where are the speed cameras? Have I got enough fuel? Where are the charge points? Are my tyres inflated and safe?

This is how you are going to approach your problems and solutions for your BestLife RoadMap. You need to look for the obstacles.

RoadMap: Navigating Your Route

Who is going to affect what you've chosen to do? Your external influences, especially for people who are recovering people pleasers, have a very, very strong pull on our actions.

I have had several clients who decided to lose weight, only to find that their partners have sabotaged them unconsciously because they do not want them to change. This is a fear response from their partners because they know, as soon as they start respecting themselves and taking responsibility for their actions, life is going to change. This triggers the fear response in that tricksy, reptilian brain.

So, if you know who will be affected by the focus you've chosen, then you've an opportunity to communicate and find a solution where you get what you want and they are satisfied with it. This way, everybody is winning, the fear response is lessened and you stand a greater chance of consistent success.

For example, my client's husband loves to bring chocolate home for her. It's his love language. And much as she loves all things sweet, they don't necessarily love her in the quantities that he brings into the house! So I suggested my client have this conversation with her husband: "I could really do with your help on my weight goal. I need to make great choices around what I'm eating, and I feel bad because I have to say no to your chocolate gifts when you are acting from a place of nurture. Could you help me, please? Instead of bringing chocolate, could you please bring me ice lollies?"

The husband still gets to bring a food gift, so they can still express their love language, and that's how they receive validation. And my client receives something that aligns with her focus and action. Everybody wins!

It is a conversation about boundaries. People hide from the difficult conversations, especially when they're people close to you. But if you are conscious of the effect your focus will have on someone in your life, you can address the issue before any negative emotions come into play on either side. This way, you set yourself up for success and communicate well about and around your decision.

By looking at the effect and possible impacts of your decision, you can plan your route to success whilst you are calm and not in a traffic jam. When traffic hits, you already have your alternative routes planned, and you are less likely to get lost and go off track.

RoadMap: Navigating Your Route

Exercise: Problems and Solutions

The point of this exercise is to give you a reference sheet for your focus, with possible problems and solutions written in one place. When you do encounter problems or you take a wrong turn, you don't have to panic and react in the moment. You are already prepared with the answers and can easily reference your ready-made solutions.

Take one of the focus actions you have chosen and write it at the top of a clean sheet of paper. Underneath, on the left-hand side, write down all the things you can think of that could go wrong or stop you from achieving this change. On the right-hand side, for each thing that could go wrong, list any possible solutions you can think of.

POSSIBLE PROBLEMS	**POSSIBLE SOLUTIONS**
_____	_____
_____	_____
_____	_____

Use quick keywords and solutions to help you avoid or reset a problem and go again. Let your brain come up with the solutions whilst you have headspace to create them. For each focus you have chosen, I suggest completing this exercise.

There will always be something that happens that you didn't think of. Chances are, because you have already done work on troubleshooting the possible problems, you will be able to look at this exercise and it will centre you enough to take emotional responses down and think more clearly about the solutions available.

Roadmap: Navigating Your Route

Internal and External Influences

External Influences

When you look at your Problems and Solutions exercise, you will see that the challenges to your focus are not always all about you, and that sometimes they're not in your control. But by looking outwards and forwards, you can plan for what your actions will be if those problems do happen.

What are those external influences? They are the people around you, the practical things you have to work around and the environment all around you.

If someone is not supportive, how will you handle it? If something is not set up to do whatever it is you have chosen to do, how can you navigate around that? If work is going to stop you from hitting your focus, how can you build your game plan around the obstacle of work? Before you set off down your chosen road, it's important to identify potential obstacles and brainstorm solutions in advance. When problems hit, pressure and stress can cloud your thinking. But if you've already done the work, you'll have solutions ready to go, helping you stay in your lane and on your BestLife route.

We discussed creating your RoadMap and breaking it down into one to three focus areas to help settle the reptilian brain and manage feelings of overwhelm. That initial pressure when you're just getting started can literally stop you in your tracks. When your brain is too full, you tend to react in an extreme way. Your fight, flight or freeze instinct can be triggered, often either going in the opposite direction or simply not doing anything! This is why, if you've done your pre-journey planning, you can choose one of your pre-planned solutions in the moment and keep moving in your chosen direction. It might work. It might not. But you have your solutions right there. You can stay calm and choose another one. This is the difference between making life choices under pressure versus making life choices in a nice, calm environment and you've got the headspace to do it.

Nobody is in control of your life other than you. You are the only one with power over your life, and it is your choice to give that power to other people. Sometimes, I still find myself going along with what other people want, just to keep the peace. So I'm not saying it's easy, but if you want real change, you have to commit. Your reptilian brain will bloody hate it, and so might the people who love you, because when you start doing something different, it threatens them as much as it threatens your brain.

Roadmap: Navigating Your Route

Being aware, up front and ahead of your journey, of how external influences can challenge the choices you've focused on can help you navigate more smoothly by preparing those who will be affected. If they know a change is coming, and why it's the best decision for you, it won't come as a shock to their reptilian brain, and they'll be less likely to react badly when it happens, because they'll have had time to prepare themselves too.

Who will you need to share your new journey with? And how will you best prepare them for the new journey?

Internal Influences

We have looked the external influences; now, you can consider your internal influences on your chosen focus. This is where you prepare, inform and embrace those two internal voices. The more you can listen to those voices and create certainty of safety and happiness in the journey, the more you will be able to stay consistent on your BestLife journey.

Your Loud Shouty Voice is going to have a field day trying to find all the reasons you need to stop the actions you are focusing on. It won't initially believe it's the right thing to do. Remember, doing the same as you always have has so far kept you safe. Your Inner Quiet Voice knows this is the right path for you to take – but you probably can't hear it when the Loud Shouty Voice is in full swing!

By acknowledging the Loud Shouty Voice and the problems it raises (it's only trying to keep you safe!), then turning to your Inner Quiet Voice and some calm, creative space, you can start finding solutions and building a case for why the change is the best thing to focus on.

Following is my game plan to help you through this process. This will get you to focus on and complete your chosen actions regularly and consistently. There are five main areas to work on. If you can get all five, or at least one of them, going in alignment with what you want to achieve, then you will be in a great place to actually live your best life according to your chosen RoadMap.

RoadMap: Navigating Your Route

Navigating your Route
Action and Course adjustments

THE PLAN

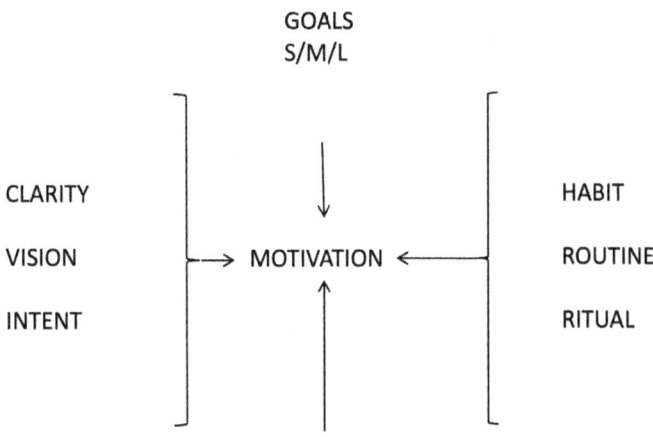

ENJOY THE JOURNEY
CELEBRATE THE
ACHIEVEMENTS

Motivation

There's a reason why it's in the middle. It's because this is the card everybody plays when change is happening: "Oh, I'm not motivated," or "I need the motivation to do this or that." But, actually, it's a load of rubbish. Motivation is about as easy to achieve as the mythical work-life balance. It's just the word that gets bandied about when you think you are responsible for difficult changes in your life.

You are responsible for the actions that you take, the focus that you make and the journey that you're on. If you get these things in alignment, the chances of you getting what you want are higher. Motivation is the word to describe a combination of actions and focuses that align with what you want to do. By creating pre-prepared actions and focuses for each of the other four sections, you will have all the motivation you need to stay on your path, to take consistent and persistent action to get you where you want to go.

Goals: S/M/L

Firstly, forgive me for bringing up the word "goals." Personally, I have rebelled against this word for years, as I have been told for years that to be "successful," I need to have my 1/5/10 year goals all planned out. Nothing brings me more horror than bringing the next ten years of my life

Roadmap: Navigating Your Route

down into an impersonal spreadsheet, an act which always seems to be the preference of people who recommend doing this! It quite literally sucks my will to live dry – *not* what my BestLife RoadMap is about.

Having said that, goals can be a great word if you can give it the personalised frame that works for you as an individual. So for me in this context, goals are the one, two or three items you have decided to focus on to help you live your BestLife. The S/M/L is the timescale that you have chosen for those focus items to happen in. By doing all the work in Parts 1 and 2 of this book, you will be able to put your focus goals into this section.

Clarity, Vision and Intent

On the left of the diagram are Clarity, Vision and Intent. I love these words as they are vital right from the start of your journey.

Get your brain bought into the change that you are focusing on, to really picture what it looks like to live that life. Being able to build a picture for each of your focus items, having clarity behind the reasons why you want this, and a clear vision of results, will all help build your intent and determination to achieve it.

I recommend creating something that resonates with you to represent your Clarity, Vision and Intent behind your BestLifeRoadMap focus items. Whatever that looks like to you. We are building the new story of your life to create certainty for your reptilian brain. After all, it does not know the difference between your actual reality and what you tell it is reality! It's why your body can feel genuine stress and anxiety in imagined difficult situations (horror films, anyone?!). By building the best picture you can of the great happiness and safety that will come from your new journey, you can reassure your reptilian brain that this change is safer than staying still, doing what you have always done.

If you are a writer, write it down. Write the story of what your life will look like during the journey and when you reach that particular destination. The more positive and evocative the language you use, the more your brain will buy into the new journey.

If you are a vision-board person, then build a vision board your way. A picture speaks a thousand words and can help you buy into change and reaffirm the reasons for your journey when it gets challenging. Visual representation, like words, has a direct line to our brains. It can be a great way to create commitment to your BestLife RoadMap. Remember, it is your vision, so choose whatever medium works for you.

RoadMap: Navigating Your Route

For a very long time, I avoided vision boards because the only ones I had seen and been encouraged to do were the cut-and-paste type. And I'm not a crafter. Looking through piles of magazines for inspiration and examples of what I wanted was soul-destroying to me. I spent the whole time fighting what I was "meant" to be doing. My Quiet Inner Voice was telling me I'm not any of those people in the magazines – I don't *want* to be any of those people. Whilst my Loud Shouty Voice told me I was failing because I couldn't even do an easy task like cutting out and sticking on! Then one day, I realised I didn't have to do it the way "they" told me to. So I used Google. With Google images, I could put in my keyword, scroll through the images until I see one that resonates, and then whack it into a PowerPoint and just create a PDF of all the pictures. Job done, no scissors or glue required!

Once you have created your version of your Clarity, Vision and Intent, you can start to use it everywhere. It is super, super powerful.

Remember, your energy flows where your focus goes.

If you place your vision story or picture somewhere you'll see it regularly, it will help keep you grounded in your focus. If there's a particular area you're finding challenging to sustain, having that story or vision visible in a positive, everyday way can really support you.

My love for off-roading trips, which do take considerable time, money, is one example. On my phone's lock screen, I have pictures of trips I've been on, especially those that really resonated with me. I bloody love them, and so every time I see them, it cements my commitment to doing what it takes to get the next one. I have my family and my dogs on there as well. Every time I pick my phone up and look at those pictures, I'm engaging with my vision.

Here's something that can be extremely powerful in helping you stay focused: find your version of it. Think about different ways you can anchor your Clarity, Vision and Intent. Use all your senses. Visual anchors might include stories or vision boards. You could choose a focus word or picture that ties your changes together. For touch, use something physical as a reminder, ideally something tactile. I wear a starfish necklace every day to connect my personal and business purposes. It's a real, tangible way to keep your focus centred on you.

By creating a strong vision and linking it to your senses, you anchor yourself to your destination. It helps you start living your BestLife now. Build the vision in your mind. Our brains don't know the difference between reality and

RoadMap: Navigating Your Route

imagination. The bigger and more positive the picture, and the more time we spend living as if we're already there, the greater the chance we have of making it real. That's what all the manifestation talk is really about: convincing your brain that this is the real and safe path.

Imagine you're going for a walk in the countryside. There's a footpath you always follow. It's well trodden, familiar and easy to navigate. This is the route you've always taken (your A to Now from Part 1). Now, off to the left, you notice something in the distance. You can't see it clearly, and there's no obvious path leading to it—but you know you want to reach it (your Now to Z from Part 2).

The destination lies beyond a field of tall grass and bushes. There's no marked route. You'll have to find your own way through. It's harder work than staying on the familiar path, but it's the way forward. This is where your route planning and solution finding come in, your RoadMap from Part 3.

The more you walk the path toward your new destination, the more comfortable it becomes. As the grass gets trodden down, the route feels easier, and the landmarks grow familiar. You have to keep working the route. This is where your Clarity, Vision and Intent start to pay off. By mentally creating the path and replaying it in your mind, your brain begins to treat it as real. Even if you haven't physically started yet, your brain will believe you have. And when you do take those first steps, your Clarity, Vision and Intent will be so well practised that your brain will feel safe – and committed – to the journey ahead.

Another way you could anchor your vision is by creating a soundtrack or a specific sound. If you're a music person, you can use a ringtone you attach to your vision. Every time your phone rings, you are able to ground yourself further into the change you want to make.

If you love a scented candle or the smell of cut grass, you might be someone who's motivated by scent. Try connecting your focus to a smell. I remember when my daughter was struggling to sleep as a child, I gave her a scarf with my perfume on it and that helped her greatly. Scent association is incredibly powerful.

If there's a smell you associate with where you want to go, use it. For years, I had a holiday in Provence on my vision board; I specifically wanted to visit the lavender fields. I finally made it happen in 2024, and it was beautiful. We did it in our own unconventional way, of course.

If this were your focus and scent was something that anchored you, carrying a sprig of lavender in your bag or pocket could be a simple but powerful way to stay connected to your goal.

Habit, Routine and Ritual

Which one of those words is most exciting?

Ritual. Are we in agreement? But the first two feed the third. And all three create the magic that is consistency.

If you take something you want to change and stack it onto something you already do, it becomes more acceptable to your brain's existing set of habits. Habit stacking simply means that the path through the field, the one we talked about under Clarity, Vision and Intent, has been broken in. With each step, that path becomes a little more familiar. You can build a habit until it becomes routine, just something you do regularly, almost without thinking.

Consistency is a key part of getting what you want. When you want to make a change in your life, creating habits can help with keeping on track. Find a small action that gets you one step towards what you want and do it every day until it feels easy and natural. Then find the next small action and stack it on top of the first. Do the first action followed by the second action until they seem easy and consistent. Then choose a third action, and so on.

For people who struggle to go to the gym and exercise, I recommend they do something small at home every day, even if it's just five squats. Choose an achievable focus habit to do consistently. Stack it on top of something else you regularly do, like boiling the kettle. This way, it is more likely to happen regularly. Once the action is a habit, it becomes easier to do five squats and a lunge whilst the kettle boils. You can literally just add one thing.

In the Problems and Solutions exercise you could ask this question: What happens to the other habits if I miss the first one? Because the actions are small, it doesn't feel like such a big deal when one slips. But often, fear of failure stops people from simply picking it back up the next day. The key is to remind yourself that the step is small, and that makes it easy to restart. When the habit is manageable, the solution is easier to find and act on.

Stopping is only a big deal when you've made your focus action so big that it's overwhelming. When you stop, it feels like a relief to your reptilian brain. It feels safer not to act, which makes it less likely you'll try again. That can leave you feeling like you've failed, like you're doomed – and like everyone who doubted you was right all along.Make the change as small as you can. Break a big change down to its

RoadMap: Navigating Your Route

smallest components. Keep it small and make it consistent and stack it to a habit that you're already doing, if you can.

The one word that connects habit and routine to consistency is ritual. Use a ritual as much as you possibly can because it triggers the reward centre in your brain. The more your brain wants to achieve your focus, the more likely your action will keep happening. Stack your actions with a series of enjoyable things, and do them every day. Once it becomes a routine, your brain feels safe and unthreatened. When the habit is firmly in place, all you need to do is start the first action in the stack. Your brain will naturally run through the sequence, visualising the end result and the reward that comes with it. Before you know it, you'll be moving along the path you want to travel with ease.

For example, if you struggle with sleep, creating your own bedtime ritual can make a big difference. Fill it with lovely, soothing things that please your senses, calm your soul, and gently signal to your brain that sleep is coming and that it's safe to relax. Practise this ritual consistently, and soon you'll notice that even starting the first step makes you feel sleepy. That's because your brain fast-forwards to the end of the routine. It knows what's coming: a good night's sleep. The predictability is reassuring, reducing anxiety and allowing the process to unfold naturally instead of resisting it. If you're a poor sleeper, give it a try!

Celebrate the Achievements

The more joy you create in the journey toward your destination, the more successful your focus will be. In my opinion, this is the most underrated and most important part of consistently living your best life. Don't get so fixated on the long-term outcome that you forget to enjoy the experience of getting there. The biggest thing that stops people from living their best life is simply not having fun along the way.

The smaller the step you take, the more likely your brain is to accept it. Nail that one small action and enjoy it. Once it feels natural and fun, it becomes part of who you are. It's just what you do. When that happens, reward yourself: read a good book, take a stroll somewhere new, enjoy a bubble bath or a swim – whatever brings you sheer enjoyment. By adding one little joyful thing to each action and giving yourself micro-rewards for staying consistent, you build a system your brain loves. Happy hormones get released, and your brain is more likely to say "yes" to the things that help you thrive. So break your one, two or three goals into tiny, manageable micro-steps. Make them as fun and easy as possible. That way, you create a reward system your reptilian brain sees as positive, safe and worth repeating.

RoadMap: Navigating Your Route

When I was going through my black 10 years of depression and I was struggling to leave the house, I would literally just stand on our doorstep and breathe the outside air. That was enough for me. My micro-action was so small that going out and standing on my porch was the win. The fresh air was my reward. My next win was walking down to the end of our driveway. Then I was walking to the first lamp post, because the win was just getting me out of the house. Fast forward to 2025 and the result of those micro-actions and more have stacked up to me being in the amazing and rewarding place of running a business helping others to do the same.

Do something about your focus every day, no matter how small. Your reptilian brain must buy into your focus changes as well in order for them to work.

Remember, where your focus goes, your energy flows.

Exercise: Visualisation and Grounding

Think about your BestLife Focus choices. How will you anchor your commitment to consistency when everyday life starts to get in the way of your focus and change?

Use the following as a guide to create your own anchors and habits, breaking your focus goals into micro actions that form the path you want to follow.

- ★ Focus on your Goals S/M/L and your micro actions

- ★ Clarity, Vision and Intent

- ★ Habit, Routine and Ritual

- ★ Celebrate your Achievements

- ★ How will you build the intentional vision of safety, joy and reward for your new path towards your destination?

- ★ Imagine your journey through stories or vision boards

- ★ Use senses as anchors (smell, touch, sound, sight, taste)

- ★ Create a series of micro-steps that are easy and bring a sense of joy and reward

RoadMap: Navigating Your Route

Answer these questions to sense check the actions you have chosen for your BestLife RoadMap.

What rituals will you need in place?

Will they fit your lifestyle?

What sacrifices or changes do you have to make?

Is your why strong enough to make changes for?

Who else will be affected?

What are the possible hurdles?

How will you deal with the hurdles?

How will you remember your why when times get hard?

Who will support you?

Part 4:
Your BestLife Journey

Just Breathe

Now is the time for action. It can be both scary and exciting at the same time. It is perfectly natural to experience conflicting emotions. The scary feeling is most likely your reptilian brain's need for reassurance. Your Loud, Shouty Voice is expressing what that part of your brain is thinking, resulting in unhelpful internal dialogue that can hold you back from starting out on the road to your BestLife. Remember, all the work you have done with this book has been to get you to this point. Your Quiet Inner Voice, if you listen, will let you know what the right thing is for you. It is exciting to start living your chosen BestLife. And you are ready!

Box Breathing

We have already established in Parts 1 to 4 that a lot goes into looking at how to live your BestLife. Your brain can find this challenging before you have even started. All the emotions will come pouring in as you move closer to taking action on the change you want in life. It can literally freeze you in place, even if you want the change *really* badly!

So now is the perfect time to bring in that key element to life: Breath. Oxygen will free your mind like nothing else. Getting a good load into your brain when you are feeling overwhelmed, scared or anxious can make the difference between action and inaction. Breath can also be the difference between action and reaction! Emotions can run very high when facing challenges. It is at those moments, before reacting, that you need to do something different. Taking a time out can be the difference between starting on your chosen road and being led down a detour not of your choosing! To help you get started, I want to introduce you to box breathing. It's a good idea to practise this technique so you can use it whenever you need a time-out whilst on your BestLife journey.

Box breathing is a useful technique when you don't know what to do, feel overwhelmed, anxious, emotional or simply feel frozen in place. It can also be used whenever you feel like your focus is being pulled away from the one, two or three BestLife Actions you've decided on. If in doubt, take a big breath!

Just Breathe

Taking control of your breath:

★ Provides vital oxygen to your brain, helping you return to a calm place to think.

★ Gives your conscious mind something other than the issue at hand to focus on.

★ Gives your subconscious a chance to process the events and provide solutions.

★ Gives you time to manage your reaction.

Giving your conscious mind a chance to process what is happening and act in your best interest is a superpower in itself. Don't let the reptilian brain run away with a knee-jerk reaction. I'm a great believer in box breathing. If you've practised and still want to take a certain action, then at least you know it is a decision you have chosen from a centred place, rather than a reaction. Once you have breathed through it, so long as it's legal, then you can choose to take that action. Choice is your power when making a change in your life. Reacting rarely helps you make the right choice for you and your BestLife. A calm, centred state of mind can rationally look at the evidence and choose. And whatever choice you make, remember that you can always make another one afterwards.

Exercise: Just Breathe

I love a bit of box breathing (also called square breathing). It is a super simple technique with super huge impact! All you have to do is imagine a box, or really, a square. Anything so long as it has four edges. As you practise this breathing technique, visualise your breath running along those four edges.

Whenever you need to, here are the steps:

1. Stop whatever it is you are doing if you can and it is safe to do so.

2. Breathe in for a count of four as you imagine yourself looking up one side of the box.

3. Hold it for four seconds as you sweep your gaze along the top edge.

4. Breathe out for another four seconds as you look down the other side of the box.

5. Hold for another four as you go along the bottom edge.

6. Repeat until calm and rational thought returns.

Your Plan, Your Action, Your Way

As you set out on your journey to live your BestLife, it is important to remember a few key things. I have gathered a quick checklist for your BestLife RoadMap before you set off.

You Are In Charge

Remember, there is only one person responsible for your life: YOU.

All actions you take in your life, you get to choose. Whether easy, hard, challenging, or whatever, they are all your choices. By knowing where you want to go, what is important to you, your agenda and your boundaries, you will be free to live and choose in total and complete alignment with your purpose and values.

You choose whether you stay on the BestLife RoadMap that you have created for yourself.

You choose whether you deviate from it.

Rate Your Life Regularly

Check in with yourself often. Choose the exercises in this book that helped you the most, and use them to check in with yourself daily. My exercise of choice is the Scores on the Doors/10 because I can choose what I am measuring and score myself easily and quickly with no need for writing or reading anything. For example, I can ask myself, "What are the scores on my doors? How happy am I in this precise moment?"

Whenever my answer is 6/10 or lower, I take that as a sign that it's time to review why that is that the case and what I need to do to get back on track.

By checking in regularly, you will be able to spot when you are being led off course, making it easier to get yourself back on the chosen road. Life will happen; things will challenge your choices and sometimes pull you hard off your road. By checking in and being vigilant over your own BestLife and happiness, you will keep making great choices whilst steering yourself around the obstacles.

Your Plan, Your Action, Your Way

Rate, Review, Reassess, Reset: Repeat the 4R's often!

Just because you've gone through this process once and created your BestLife RoadMap doesn't mean it will serve you forever.

Life will always change. That's what makes it exciting.

I have created this RoadMap and these exercises so that you can continually check that you are still on the right road for you.

I would suggest keeping a BestLife folder and diarying time and pace away from your life regularly to check that it is all still working for you. Choose a specific timescale. Some people like a yearly review. Others have a 12-week cycle. Others check in with their folder anytime their BestLife Score on the Door gets below a 6/10 (this is me!).

Remember, just because you made one decision doesn't mean you can't change your course by making another.

As my mammy said to me once, "Yes, you make your bed and you lie in it. Doesn't mean you can't change the sheets!"

Your Energy Flows Where Your Focus Goes

Know where you want to go and how you will get there. Be clear about what you want and the micro-steps that will take you there.

Keep your anchors to focus close at hand; let them act as regular reminders of why you want this life.

Create your rituals around your habits. Create routine actions to help your reptilian brain feel safe and secure with the changes. Consistent action always beats relying on motivation!

Bestlife Roadmap Wrap-Up

So we come to the end of this journey together. Thank you for giving your precious time to this book. I have loved writing my BestLife RoadMap. I made it for you to create and live the best version of your life.

The BestLife RoadMap will keep you on your own path to a thriving and happy life. If used regularly, it will ensure that you constantly move along your road with purpose and happiness. It will help you move towards your dreams through achievable and sustainable actions.

To recap your BestLife RoadMap, I've broken it up into simple prompts for ease of reference below. There is also a list of the exercises that help you find your way.

BestLife RoadMap

A to Z of Life: Who are you?

A to Now: Where have you come from?

Now: Where are you now?

Now to Z: Where do you want to go?

RoadMap: How are you going to get there?

The Journey: How do you keep moving in the right direction?

Go: Time to take the first step!

As we reach the end of the journey through your Best Life RoadMap, it is time to see how far you have come. Below is a little recap for you to remember where you started on this journey with me. Maybe you picked up this book because you were unhappy or dissatisfied with your life, with how it looked and felt. Maybe you weren't thriving or even doing anything for yourself and your own happiness because you were too busy doing all the things for all the people. Maybe you had been doing the same things over and over and had no idea what your life could be like with

BestLife Roadmap Wrap-Up

a bit of fun, excitement or adventure. Perhaps fear kept you in place, and so you stayed safe, with no disruptions and an "easy" life. Now, at the final stage of this book, you must be excited and raring to go out and live your BestLife fully.

You have clarity on who you are and what makes you happy, what you want to achieve and how and by when.

You have a plan for what you want to focus on immediately and a RoadMap of your BestLife.

You know the 4 R's to regularly review, rate, renew and reset so that you stay on track for life consistently.

You have the framework to assess whether your priorities change and whether a new direction is required. You have the ability to implement and travel your new route and navigate the detours.

You have your Inner Quiet Voice to help you manage and reassure your Load Shouty Voice and your reptilian brain.

You have problem-solving skills and the ability to take necessary actions around roadworks that internal and external influences cause. You have the plan to take responsibility for and the skills to live your Best Life.

Exercise:
My RoadMap for My BestLife

What an exciting and empowering journey it has been and will continue to be. Stick to your path and your RoadMap will guide your way. Let's create a summary page for your BestLife. This will make it easier to refer back and check in with your progress

My BestLife RoadMap

	1	2	3
My theme is			
My chosen focus items are			
My time scale for each is			
I am focusing on these because			

BestLife Roadmap Wrap-Up

	1	2	3
The difference this will make to my life is			
My Clarity/Vision/Intent is represented by			
My Senses Anchor to my *why* is			
My first Micro Step/Actions are			
My problem/solutions are			
I will celebrate my achievements by			
My next 4R's RoadMap Review is on			

Bonus Time:

What have you learned about you and your BestLife on the journey through this book?

What has surprised you?

What didn't you know about yourself?

What have you chosen to action?

What does life look like for you moving forward down the road?

When have you diarised your next BestLife Review to happen?

What Happens Next?

And that is us at the end of this particular road.

It only remains for me to wish you bon voyage on your most epic, healthy and happy BestLife!

The magic of you and your purpose needs to be released into this world.

I wish you your Best Life for each and every step on your chosen journey!

You have the roadmap and skills to continually and consistently live the BestLife that you chose, so go out and consistently choose to live it!

Remember: Your energy flows where your focus goes. Your choice, your life, your way.

The Complete Set of RoadMap Exercises

Here are all the exercises within the book for you to easily find and use.

Brain Dump Mind Map - Everything You Do	42
In and Out of The Box	56
What is Important to You?	75
Scores on The Doors/10	96
Your Current Road Marker	104
Your Position Now On Your A to Z of Life	117
The Good, the Bad, the Ugly	123
Create and Keep Your Agenda	136
Find Your Filters	159
Story Time	184
Lost and Found and Hopes and Dreams	195
Destination Summary	203
Traffic-Light Your Life	215

What Happens Next?

Choose Your RoadMap Route	227
Problems and Solutions	237
Visualisation and Grounding	256
Just Breathe	264
My RoadMap for My BestLife	272

Further Support

If you have any questions or would like to know more, please use the following resources that I have set up to support you. Below is a QR code that leads to The Southey Way website.

Join the "SOS Your Life" WhatsApp group for ongoing and regular posts from us and support from our community.

Subscribe to our "A Story with…" newsletter for topics about life and health.

Join our SOS Life Academy or SOS Health Academy for focused support and accountability.

Social Media

You can engage with us by following us on our The Southey Way social media pages.

LinkedIn

Sara Southey: https://www.linkedin.com/in/sarasouthey

The Southey Way: https://www.linkedin.com/company/the-southey-way/

Facebook

https://www.facebook.com/TheSoutheyWay

Instagram

https://www.instagram.com/the_southey_way

Tiktok

https://www.tiktok.com/@the_southey_way

Review and Feedback

I am always interested in learning how people utilise the BestLife RoadMap and what changes and adaptations they make. Please let me know how your life changes from this moment on.

Acknowledgements

I've had this book on my vision board ever since I started The Southey Way in 2016.

Gratitude and thanks go to so many people who have come into my life for a reason, a season and for life.

Special mention goes to my husband Jim, who, although not in the personal development world, supports me on my mission to help the world live healthier, happier lives. You are the shipping forecast for my storms.

Huge gratitude to my fabulous adult children, Ben and Jenny, who show me there is always something new to learn and different ways of living and approaching life. May you always be this open-minded and tolerant of the close-minded thinkers! I am so proud of you both.

To my brilliant Southey Way Superstars, you continue to inspire me to give my best to support you and others like you. You are the reason I love what I do. Without you, this book would not exist. You helped me create the RoadMap to your BestLife by feeling safe enough to trust me to help you live your best lives. The way we have worked together has helped shape the framework for this book. Thank goodness for you.

To my fabulous network of friends, both personal and professional, your help and support continue to enable me to continue on my own BestLife Journey and deliver on my purpose to help the world thrive, one person at a time.

People come into your life for a reason, a season or for life (or all three), and I constantly learn about myself from the joys and challenges that relationships bring. I'm not going to name you as I know I would miss someone vital, but you know who you are and I feel blessed to have you in my life.

www.ingramcontent.com/pod-product-compliance
Lightning Source LLC
Chambersburg PA
CBHW050337010526
44119CB00049B/586